Palazzi of Sicily

Angheli Zalapì

Palazzi of Sicily

Introduction
Gioacchino Lanza Tomasi

Photographs
Melo Minnella

KÖNEMANN

Copyright © 1998
Arsenale Editrice,
Venice, Italy

Original title: *Dimore di Sicilia*

Copyright © 2000 for the English edition
Könemann Verlagsgesellschaft mbH
Bonner Strasse 126, D–50968 Cologne

Translation from Italian: Elizabeth Clegg,
Laura Davey and Alexandra Trone in
association with G&E 2000 Ltd
Editing: Karen May in association with
G&E 2000 Ltd
Typesetting: G&E 2000 Ltd, Cambridge
Project Management: Jackie Dobbyne in
association with G&E 2000 Ltd
Project Coordination: Nadja Bremse
Production: Ursula Schümer
Printing and binding: Imprimerie Jean
Lamour, Maxéville

Printed in France

ISBN 3-8290-3449-0

10 9 8 7 6 5 4 3 2 1

The photographs on pages 13, 28, 56, 84
and 126 are published thanks to the kind
permission of Cesare Barbera.

To Irene

Ti saluto, o terra amatissima,
che ho preferito al cielo:
a te affido l'orgoglio
del mio sangue e la mia gioia

[I greet this much beloved land
that I prefer to heaven itself:
and give to it all the pride
of my blood and all my joy]

Cerere's Homage to Sicily
C. Claudianus (370–408),
De Raptu Proserpinae, Book I,
verses 185–187.

Angheli

Contents

Origins and evolution of palazzi in Sicily

Any account tracing the origins and evolution of palatial residences in Sicily must begin with the imposing Roman villas of the fourth century AD. The best known is that of Piazza Armerina although similar buildings have also been found near Patti, in the province of Messina, and at Tellaro, south of Syracuse. The evidence of this style of villa, in the latter days of the Roman Empire before the Vandal invasion, reveals that Sicily derived its enormous prosperity from agriculture. Indeed, so great was the island's wealth that its large landowners chose to live on their own estates. In the first century AD, Vitruvius described in detail a "Greek-style" dwelling in Hellenistic Sicily. The entire building faced inwards and was built around two peristyles (colonnaded garden courts). This arrangement can be seen in the larger houses of the Morgantina area, including the Magistrate's House. Yet all that remains of these buildings is the ground plan. However, if we compare these fourth-century villas with the Norman–Arab pleasure palaces, there is a thread of continuity linking the owners and the environment. All these residences use architecture and furnishings to construct a dialogue between man and nature. Artificial spaces are created which are used to allay tension and which weave a kind of magic. This is yet another example of how Islamic influences have affected Classical culture. When, in Baghdad, the basic plan of the basilica was adapted to become a mosque, this modification was then repeated along the shores of the Mediterranean, an area particularly receptive to the opposing influences of Europe and the East.

Norman rule

The thirteenth-century Castello di Maredolce and other pleasure palaces constructed under Norman rule were typical of the new type of residential building found in this southerly kingdom. The Arabic for castle is Qasr Ga'far, after its founder, the Emir Ga'far (967–1019). Ibn Gubayr described the castle in a diary based on his journey from Valencia to Mecca. The placename Maredolce (sweet water) is derived from the huge freshwater pool that surrounds the castle on three sides. All that exists of this today is a section of the pozzuolana hydraulic system and, at the foot of Mount Grifone, the arches that once piped in water from the spring. Arab technology for water features and water gardens was incorporated in all the pleasure palaces of the Norman period. These include Zisa, Cuba, the Alfaina Tower or Cuba Soprana in the park of Villa Napoli, and Uscibene or Mimmermo. All these castles and palaces were built during the reign of William, in the second half of the twelfth century.

Pleasure palaces were different from other palaces. The most important of these was the Castello Superiore, now known simply as the Palazzo dei Normanni. This was re-built by Roger II on the foundations of an earlier fortress. Excavation has shown that, over the centuries, the site of the castle had continuously been the seat of military power, starting with the Carthaginians and then the Romans. The Emir abandoned the castle in 937, moving his court to Kalsa, *al-Halisah* (the elect), a new fortified citadel erected next to the sea. From the palace, the royal park, the Genoardo, extended down to the Palazzi del Parco and Monreale at the far end of the valley. In between was the Conca d'Oro with its pleasure palaces. Some of these buildings have long disappeared and now only archeological sites are left. Throughout the centuries other palaces, in particular Palazzo dei Normanni and Palazzo Zisa, maintained a public or residential role, exerting the kind of fascination reserved for homes that have been lived in over the ages. In common with its architecture and town planning, residential buildings in Palermo unquestionably fell under the influence of the East well into the Norman–Hofenstaufen era. It would, indeed, have probably been very difficult to distinguish between the lifestyles of the Norman rulers and their aristocracy and those of the emirs who preceded them. On the other hand, a similar period of transformation had occurred in Frankish–Provençal feudalism during the occupation of Jerusalem. The Franks assimilated the way of dressing, customs and behaviour of the Semite peoples around them.

Multi-ethnic living survived for almost a century in Sicily despite all the barriers of language and religion that had been established. It was this strong multi-ethnicity that underpinned the financial and political success of the Kingdom of Sicily. Palermo was a city of 100,000 inhabitants, second in size only to Constantinople in the Western world. The Eastern customs practised in the city included polygamy and the allocation of space for harem quarters was usual in domestic buildings throughout the Christian East from S. Giovanni d'Acri to Constantinople. Palermo's Palazzo dei Normanni built under Norman and Hohenstaufen (Swabian) rulers is no exception. Apart from the capital, no other town in Sicily had more than 10,000 inhabitants. However, a recent discovery has shown that the architectural trend towards building pleasure palaces was not limited only to the capital. Proof of this is provided in *Il Castello di Caronia* published by Walter Kroenig. The symmetrical layout of the royal palace and the way air circulates inside the building via pipes which run down from the towers is the same as that of Palazzo Zisa. Such sophisticated air-conditioning technology reveals much about Islamic scientific culture and appears to indicate a level of architectural design expertise unknown in the Western world at that time. The goal of Islamic architecture was to construct an earthly representation of the Koranic concept of heaven. This was accomplished by the use of water features, artificial breezes and enclosed spaces which created the impression of being open and captivating thanks to the repeated use of symmetry. Palaces like the Zisa or the Alhambra harnessed artistic creativity to the service of pleasure, disregarding all thoughts of penitence and ambition. The culture of pleasure palaces declined under the Hohenstaufens. Frederick II was forced to neglect the pearl of his kingdom and to sacrifice the composite roots of his culture to further his imperialist dreams. Multi-ethnicity suffered and the multi-lingual monarch, known as *Stupor Mundi* (the Wonder of the World), who grew up in the park of Palazzo Genoardo, implemented a plan to repress the Muslims. He ultimately unleashed a series of bitter religious wars with the intention of bringing Sicily firmly back under Western control.

From the Sicilian Vespers (1282) to the Peace of Caltabellotta (1302) Sicily was gripped by an iron rule and, from this period on, the two shores of the Mediterranean would never again be culturally united. Although suppressed, the old longing for comfort did occasionally resurface in the culture of Sicilian towns in the form of the country houses of the Renaissance described by Di Giovanni, the sultry chambers and the languid pleasures of Giacomo Serpotta's theatre, to the flattery of rocaille, the Gothic Revival and eventually to Art Nouveau, known locally as Liberty Style.

Fourteenth and fifteenth centuries: Gothic and Catalan Sicily

Palazzo dei Normanni is among a number of buildings that symbolize a city whose shifts in taste became integrated into the very fabric of its structures. These buildings reveal the existence of an enduring mission. The palaces built in the fourteenth and fifteenth centuries, on the other hand, are merely episodic illustrations of Sicily under the rule of the Hohenstaufens, Aragonese and Catalans. And yet the fact that the island came under the Catalan sphere of influence nonetheless had a dramatic effect. Sicily only really caught up with the Renaissance when the sixteenth century was already well advanced.

During the fourteenth century the House of Aragon ruled Sicily, but wielded no real power. As rulers with no fixed abode, these monarchs were forced to make deals with the island's mighty feudal families. They wandered from one castle to the next, without the authority to demand basic taxes from the people. It is due to these peregrinations that the main reception room in historic Sicilian homes of that time became known as the barons' chamber, since parliamentary meetings were held there by rulers who had no centre of government of their own. On the death of Frederick IV, known as Frederick the Simple, the throne passed to his daughter Maria. In reality, however, power fell into the hands of four regents, creating a climate which was fraught with melodrama.

It was hardly surprising then that fortified mansions soon sprang up in both feudal territories and towns. In Palermo these included Palazzo Chiaramonte (built around 1320 according to Fazello) and Palazzo Sclafani (1330). Frederick II of Aragon's castle at Montalbano Elicona was built after the 1302 Peace of Caltabellotta. Caccamo, Mussomeli, Misilmeri, Cefalà, Castronovo, Sutera, Favara and Naro are all dominated by castles built by Manfred III, a member of the Chiaramonte family. In 1316 Francis I, from the rival Sicilian clan, the powerful Ventimiglia family, set up home in Castelbuono. Halfway through the fourteenth century, the Moncada family restored the stronghold at Paternò. When the Catalans seized power in 1392, they rewarded those who had fought for them with property taken from the supporters of the losing side (the Angevins or Latins). Martin the Younger gave the castle at Carini' to the Grua-

Talamancas. The castle had been built by Rudolph Bonello, a warrior who had fought with Count Roger during his Sicilian campaign. The castle then passed to the Abbate family, one of the most important on the Angevin side, and then to the Grua Talamancas. In all of these buildings, and indeed in all buildings constructed up until the middle of the sixteenth century, the identity of Sicily is shaped by its historical origins. Gradually craftsmen began to shift away from the Mediterranean Islamic style. Florence seemed a million miles away when, around 1480, the Ajutamicristo and Abatellis families commissioned Matteo Carnilivari to construct their new town mansions. At about the same time, the Bellomo family refurbished its palazzo in Syracuse and Palazzo Steripinto was being built in Sciacca. This occurred while the Humanist style of the Renaissance first filtered into Sicily, thanks mainly to the arrival of sculptors trained in the north. They included Francesco Laurana and the Gagini family from Bissone, who started a tradition which was to last for over two centuries. Their work can still be seen in tombs and in

Gothic was still flourishing. Indeed, in the same period the finishing touches were being made to the Palazzo Termine Pietratagliata and the castle at Carini. In turn the ceiling of the so-called Barons' Chamber at Carini inspired the refurbishment of the ceiling at Pietratagliata.

The very notion of a castle court life within the town demonstrates quite clearly how independent the barons were. The construction of Palazzo Sclafani and Palazzo Steri changed the road layout of Palermo. The fortified mansions were encircled by walls and protected from the outside world by a broad buffer zone of orchards and kitchen gardens. These buffer zones were to disappear in later centuries as the town expanded. What little remained of them before the Second World War has now been eaten away by illegal building developments in the suburbs. This is certainly what happened to the Torre dei Diavoli which was part of the Steri park. To some extent, the mansions represented a further progression from the "heaven-on-earth" created at Genoardo and the later style of villa homes. The taste for court living never completely disappeared. Indeed it continued to resurface in Palermo until the end of the nineteenth century. Between the fourteenth and fifteenth centuries, Sicilian artistic culture in towns demonstrated a marked tendency towards provincial courtliness. The most important work in this context is a huge cycle of paintings at Palazzo Steri that Manfred III of Chiaramonte commissioned between 1377 and 1380. Throughout the fourteenth century the whole area of influence was decidedly Mediterranean, Catalan and Provençal right down to the type of painting that was imported. Things were different in the countryside, where the fortresses were completely rooted in the territory that made up their power base. From time to time these strongholds would be visited by the wandering court of the Sicilian Aragonese rulers. These kings, who had no seats, held parliaments in Palazzo Corvaja in Taormina or in other fortresses of which only the walls still stand. It was at Mussomeli that in 1391 Andrea Chiaramonte called the barons together in an attempt to fend off a Catalan re-conquest of the island. The castle, which stands on a rocky outcrop some distance from the village of the same name, is the one surviving ruin that best evokes the spirit of the Chiaramonte family. Their lives were lived in fortresses and blighted by their tenuous grasp on power.

Madonnas all over Sicily. The first outside influence to reach Sicily was that of the Renaissance, which was shortly followed by Mannerism. The effect was to provoke a clash of cultures which lasted until midway through the sixteenth century. The clash was initially resolved by the arrival of a number of religious Orders. These Orders, especially the Jesuits, had a predilection for buildings constructed around a central area. When ecclesiastical intellectuals came to the island, a nucleus of architects was established which worked on the Senate in Palermo. These architects were all professionals, well-informed of the prevailing ideas, and who had, in the main, been trained in Rome. Even though examples of Tuscan influence are not unknown, in the early part of the sixteenth century they must have stood out, to say the least. One such example is Palazzo Agnello in Via dell' Incoronazione, which is almost a replica of the Sacra Casa di Loreto transported to Palermo at the start of the century and at a time when Catalan

The power of the Chiaramonte family waned after Andrea was beheaded in 1392. Nonetheless, for the next two centuries a section of Sicilian nobility continued to live in these feudal strongholds, which have now completely gone. Towards the end of the sixteenth century Renaissance culture flowered and took root on the island. This can also be seen from the feudal courts of western Sicily. In towns like Taormina, Randazzo, Piazza Armerina and Naro a new stability developed, which had a knock-on effect on urban construction, which now tended towards smaller mansions and houses for the middle classes. The start of this stability can be traced to the reign of Alfonso V of Aragon, also called "The Magnanimous". It was thanks to his standing and patronage of the arts that the manners of mainland Italian courts were able to gain a foothold on the island. Poetry written in Palermo by sixteenth-century Humanists and madrigals composed by the Sicilian polyphonic school link Sicily to

the artistic civilization of the major cities on the Italian peninsula. Figures such as the poet Antonio Veneziano, the musician Pietro Vinci, the architect Matteo Carnilivari rank highly alongside Antonello da Messina in reshaping the face of Sicilian culture at the start of the sixteenth century.

The best example of this blossoming is Palazzo Ajutamicristo, Carnilivari's masterpiece of civil architecture. But this zest for life also spread into the countryside, as we can see from Pietro Speciale's first plans for the castle at Ficarazzi. He had built a palace, now Palazzo Raffadali, in Palermo, when he was *Pretore* (Chief Justice). Towards the end of the fifteenth century he started building what is now the Palazzo Pretorio (Palace of Justice). Like the castle at Ficarazzi, these buildings were later refurbished to suit the new Mannerist taste. Ficarazzi was converted towards the middle of the eighteenth century by the Giardina family, who by then were known as the principi di

Ficarazzi. It contains some of the most striking settings found in a country mansion. The castle itself was hidden behind a Baroque curtain wall and a huge staircase connects the fifteenth-century fabric to ground level. Its ramp is unquestionably one of the most unusual entrances of any country villa in the Bagheria area.

The arrival of Mannerism. Sicily, outpost of the western Mediterranean

The political changes that took place at the outset of the sixteenth century mark the beginning of Sicily's move to a central position in Spanish international interests. More particularly it was crucial to their interests in the western Mediterranean. Tension with the world of Islam was mounting after the Ottoman expansion that followed the fall of Constantinople. This international threat meant that all Sicilian towns and cities were now fortified and became part of a larger political and military game. Military engineers were brought in by both the Spanish and the religious Orders of the Counter Reformation. By now these were established in every town in Sicily. Together the government and the Orders implemented a series of town planning initiatives that

were to change the face of the island. Sicily became part of Spanish Italy. Planning was in the hands of professionals who were past masters in the twin arts of war and fortification. The roots of their craft went right back to the Tuscan engineers of the Renaissance who designed public works as well as civil and military projects. They had produced names such as Taccola, Francesco di Giorgio Martini and Leonardo da Vinci. The Spanish engineers made their first appearance in Messina, where they were responsible for introducing the fashion for architectural set pieces. The most striking example of this is the palisade on the Strait. They then moved on to Palermo and Trapani. As they fanned out through Sicily, so did Tuscan ideas of perspective used in art, of mathematical planning and of new social values. Sicilian society was to be radically changed by this. Town planning and architecture came together to provide a unified vision of Baroque. When Val di Noto was hit by an earthquake in 1693, new artistic and juridical parameters had to be drawn up that would facilitate reconstruction. Sicily became the test case for Filarete's town planning theories. Two centuries after Renaissance engineers first advanced their theories, whole new villages were

built based on their notions of geometry and radial patterns around a central point. The results can be seen from Grammichele to Santo Stefano, the feudal estate of the Duca Lanza di Camastra, who had been put in charge of reconstructing the flattened area.

Sixteenth-century mansions

Mannerism directly replaced the taste for Catalan Gothic, without the usual intermediate step of pure Renaissance architecture. Sicily missed out on this altogether with the exception of Palazzo Agnello in Via dell'Incoronazione in Palermo. Although the home of minor aristocracy, it is nevertheless fascinating because the façade could have been plucked straight from the banks of the Arno in Pisa. The most important sixteenth-century houses surrounding Palermo are Villa Belvedere at Mezzo-monreale and Palazzo Castrone Santa Ninfa at the approach to the cathedral. The former is simple and classical, understated in comparison to the palazzo with its three-tiered façade interrupted by an embossed Mannerist doorway and a Serlian loggia.

During this period there was also a revival of interest in villas in the Conca d'Oro. Apart from Villa Belvedere, which was originally commissioned by Luca Pollastra, Secretary of State under John of Aragon in the mid-fifteenth century, all the other villas have now disappeared. All that remains are the descriptions penned by the Humanists of the day, from which it would appear that the villas were probably more influenced by the Classical ideal than is generally thought. The first generation of fifteenth-century Sicilian-based Humanists who knew the courts of Italy included Panormita, Tudisco and Aurispa and were succeeded in the following century by Antonio Veneziano and Tommaso Fazello. Charles of Aragon, Duca di Terranova, owned a villa known as "Le quattro camere" (Four Rooms). He was viceroy from 1566–68, during which time the Cassaro was extended as far as the sea and Piazza Bologni was opened up. Further back stood Villa La Nave, owned by the Ventimiglia family. The magnificent water features of the villa were first lauded when Leandro Alberti passed through Sicily in 1526 and later by Veneziano's panegyric on Francesco Camilliani's newly built fountain in Piazza Pretoria, which the Palermo Senate had

cabinet-making that survive nearly all date from the early seventeenth century. The succession of architects who worked on the Senate in Palermo almost all had ecclesiastical backgrounds and in the early years a number were brought in from Rome. Their influence can be seen in the design of furniture, gold artefacts and decorations. The transition from the Lombard architect Giulio Lasso, who designed the Teatro del Sole, and Palermo-born Mariano Smiriglio, who completed the façade of the Quattro Canti, happened over a single decade. Smiriglio took an interest in virtually all aspects of the project, establishing a working practice that was to be continued for a couple of centuries by all other architects who worked on the Palermo Senate.

Mannerism and Baroque in Sicily

During the seventeenth century, the most notable trend in Sicilian buildings was conformity. The whole of society appeared to be gripped by a building frenzy on both state-owned land and in the newly established feudal estates. Public or large-scale buildings had to conform to the town plans. Increasingly, architects and planners strove to achieve theatrical sweeps of perspective. Buildings and society reflected one another quite happily. One illustration of this was the monumental continuity of the compact skyline, originally fashioned by the way the main roads cut the towns in two – as in the case of Via Maqueda or the Messina palisade. Another is the way in which, as was happening right across Europe, towns began to spread into the surrounding countryside. The trends embodied the age of absolute monarchy epitomized by Versailles. In this context, Sicily's isolation from other European sources of reference frequently led to trends being expressed in a succession of different idioms. The hallmark of stately homes in Sicily at this time was therefore their very diversity. Clearly, this diversity was felt more keenly in the provinces where baronial palazzi were built on feudal estates such as Roccavaldina, Palma di Montechiaro or Aragona. Each of the three examples is completely different and yet all three are similar, almost as if they were three different sketches by the same *vedutista*. Another major influence on such palazzi could well have been the idiosyncratic behaviour of the aristocrats who commissioned them. There was, for instance, Giulio Tomasi who, in the

bought from Tuscany in 1573. Villa Tasca Lanza di Camastra, originally built by Aloisio da Bologna, dates from midway through the century. Then, at the end of the century, the Palermo town planners decided to slice the city in half by building Via Maqueda. This created the crossroads at the Teatro del Sole (generally known as Quattro Canti) which soon became a meeting place from which the city was to draw its life blood.

The architects and sculptors arriving in Sicily at this time all came from Tuscany. However, throughout the sixteenth century, the island proved resistant to Renaissance painting. Right up to the end of the century Sicily continued to commission Flemish paintings and to import works of art from the Catalan–Provençal area. Sicilians had long been familiar with this type of art and the habit of looking to these places for works of art was encouraged because they all existed within the same realm of Spanish European influence. The Low Countries were a key economic component of this.

Almost no furnishings and decorations from this era exist now. The rare examples of gold artefacts, fabrics, furniture and second half of the seventeenth century, installed a cubicle representing the Sacred House of Loreto in one of the reception rooms of his palace. Then in Aragona, Palazzo Naselli was turned into a replica of a mansion from the Castelli Romani, probably the work of Milanese ecclesiastical architect Giuseppe Mariani who was responsible for Villa Cutò in Bagheria. This villa was inspired by mansions in contemporary Rome, modelled on Villa Altieri or possibly Villa Doria Pamphili. In the same vein, Palazzo di Roccavaldina was refurbished in a grandly Mannerist way. The palazzo had originally been designed at the end of the sixteenth century by Andrea Valdina who came from an Aragonese military family with over two centuries of public service.

At Roccavaldina, the airy inner portico is the vernacular incarnation of the Mannerism of Michelangelo. As such, it is typical of buildings in Messina at a time when Andrea Calamech from Carrara dominated the local architectural scene. Back in the capital, however, the same characteristics inspired the large-scale residential building projects in Bagheria. The fashion was started by Giuseppe Branciforte, Conte di Raccuia, who built himself a house in Bagheria sometime between 1658 and 1682. Giuseppe Branciforte considered himself to be politically persecuted and withdrew to Bagheria in voluntary exile. His mansion included a number of Hispanic features, including a large frieze framing a bust of Branciforte himself, located at the top of the flight of steps on the façade. Another Hispanic notion was to place two Mannerist towers overlooking the entrance to the courtyards in front of the main elevation of the mansion. This type of playful reference to military architecture originally came from country mansions around Rome. Conceits of power more in keeping with a provincial magnate than a Renaissance prince appear in San Marco at Villa Filangeri, attributed to the priest-architect Andrea Cirrincione. Because the families have continued to live in villas, they have also been continually modernized. For example, frescoed false ceilings were in vogue in the eighteenth century, while in the seventeenth the fashion was to embellish the real ceilings, usually rustic coffers, painted in tempera, with ornamental designs and then round them off with a frescoed frieze between the ceiling and the walls. This, in fact, was a typical motif used in Rome during the sixteenth century and Villa De Simone-Wirz in Partanna contains some beautifully preserved examples. In Palermo, the older coffered ceilings can often be found underneath the later false ceilings which were mainly installed with a view to better separating spaces and differentiating between the rooms. This was because in the eighteenth century people began to assign specific uses to the various rooms thus ending the open use of space that had been encouraged by having a series of square rooms leading into each other.

Villas and country houses

The fashion for country villas was a prelude to a taste for life inspired by Rousseau. This was to reach Palermo at the close of the eighteenth century, namely the end of the century of Enlightenment. However, as far as Sicily was concerned, this had never really come about. Now the trend manifested itself in the wholesale conversion of existing rural buildings and, less often, in the building of larger villas from scratch. A typical example of the former is Villa Niscemi in the Colli plains. Here conversion work consisted of adding two broad terraces, which probably indicates the intention to install some kind of external staircase. In fact, Villa Niscemi was never finished during the eighteenth century. Of that era, all that remain are a few frescoed reception rooms on the *piano nobile* (reception floor) with lovely courtly paintings in the popular style which are also found in the neighbouring Villa Pantelleria and Villa Spina, dating from around the same time. During the following two centuries, much attention was lavished on Villa Niscemi, which was refurbished repeatedly in tune with the constant urge to improve the quality of life. In the 1930s a terrible fire devastated the villa and several rooms had to be repainted. They were then refurbished after the Second World War from plans drawn by Gino Morici. It is to him that we owe the design of the furnishings in the dining room, the repainting of the barrel-vaulted ceiling and the portrait of the Kings of Sicily in the entrance.

Courtly villas and palazzi in the eighteenth century

In the eighteenth century, large official villas made up an entire chapter in the history of social life in Palermo. Over the course of a hundred years they managed to embody the ambitions of

Left
The church and former convent
of S. Benedetto in Militello
Val di Catania
(Catania).

libri di feste (festival books) and the early guides to the island. In this context, from 1686 onwards a pamphlet was published each year for the Feast of Santa Rosalia. The pamphlets' illustrations provide a two-hundred year record of changes in fashion. Arcangelo Leanti included two of the largest villas in Palermo in his first digest dedicated to the delights of Sicily. The houses chosen were Villa Valguarnera in Bagheria and Villa Napoli Resuttano on the Piana dei Colli. They were featured among a number of large eighteenth-century country parks laid out with kitchen gardens and woodlands where pavilions and belvederes completed the setting. In the first half of the eighteenth century, three important *libri di feste* were published. Two of them featured Victor Amadeus of Savoy and Charles III of Bourbon riding from the harbour through Porta Felice. Other plates illustrate how the city was decorated, the firework scaffolding erected in the harbour and the original building of the huge Palazzo Branciforte Butera next to the harbour.

Guarino Guarini and Filippo Juvarra, who both started working for Victor Amadeus of Savoy during his reign in Sicily, were both very active in and around Messina. The two leading architects in Palermo, Paolo Amato and Giovan Battista Amico, both published tracts in which they explained their vision of architecture. By the use of perspective, they aimed to bring out the best in the urban environment. In and around Palermo, the practical outcome of their speculative activity can be seen in a group of eighteenth-century buildings – Villa Valguarnera and Villa Palagonia in Bagheria and in town Palazzo Gangi, Palazzo Villafranca, Palazzo Comitini, Palazzo Sant'Elia, Palazzo Cutò – and the seventeenth-to-eighteenth-century conversion of Palazzo Mazzarino. In these houses the interior decoration adopts the idea of large-scale architectural illusions so popular in Europe at the time. Above all, in Palazzo Gangi, this type of decoration is particularly strong on the double-lined ballroom ceiling, where the effect is reminiscent of the work of the Viennese master of this art, Johann Fischer von Erlach, Superintendent of Imperial Buildings. Such virtuoso renderings, which derived directly from Baciccia's pictorial illusionism, melded stucco and fresco work seamlessly. Pictures, with foreshortened figures, came tumbling over the edges. Amico described it his treatise and it was applied in Palazzo Gangi by

this period of peace which began after the end of the War of the Spanish Succession and was brought to an abrupt end by the Napoleonic Wars. Together with the palazzi of the same period, they possibly represent the apex of Sicilian civil culture. Visitors arriving on the island from the middle of the eighteenth century onwards described Sicily as an old society, which shunned trade and was on the sidelines of the problems of mainland Europe. The visitors themselves were attracted there by the ruins of Hellenistic Sicily which, at the time, were the only remains easily accessible to a curious Classicist. The vogue for Classics was to remain strong from the Enlightenment right through to Winckelmann and beyond. Erudite scholars who had trained in Germany wrote treatises on its political sociology, but people who felt they truly belonged to European civilization knew Sicily above all from extensive folios of etchings. These magnificent volumes were masterpieces produced by the French publishing houses of the day. The south of Italy was portrayed as a distant and magical place in pastoral scenes painted by a team of artists sent down by the abbot of Saint Non. A slightly more modern illustration of the island, heavily influenced by *La Nouvelle Héloïse*, appeared in a large, four-volume folio by Jean Houel. In the meantime, local publishers started to produce volumes which often concentrated on the island's natural beauties. The same applied to what were termed his disciple Andrea Gigante. On the other hand, something similar to this had already been tried in the ceiling frescoes of the main reception room in Palazzo Mazzarino, painted by Gaspare Serenario. The effect, however, was later destroyed when the room was partitioned. The same artists also used Illusionism on the ballroom ceiling in Palazzo Villafranca. All this was part of a fantastical universe that had started at the turn of the century in the mature works of Giacomo Serpotta.

The fact that aristocrats were busy building such imposing palaces should not, however, be taken for a sign of real economic stability among the ruling class. Rather it reflects the illusion of eternity of which Prince Salina speaks [in *The Leopard*] as he contemplates the vast ceiling in Palazzo Ponteleone. In fact, the construction techniques used on these mansions, especially the country ones, were such that they were quite unable to sustain any illusion whatsoever about how long they would last. After a couple of generations the foundations gave way and the rubble-filled walls split open like pomegranates. The ensuing work, needed to make good the structural shortcomings shared by all these buildings, coincided with a shift in taste. The entire image system reflected in the furnishings of these homes and the layout of their park was scrapped and re-invented from scratch.

One feature all the homes in question have in common is that they were first conceived at the height of the Rococo period and finished in Vanvitelli's style. Construction itself usually took about fifty years to complete, time enough to rethink the original design criteria more than once. For this reason, very few places seem to possess a unitary integrity. In Palazzo Gangi, for example, apart from the light fittings, only the ballroom design was done with a single vision, from the Louis XVI furnishings to the battle scenes on the tiled floor and the fresco showing the *Trionfo della fede* (Triumph of Faith) painted by Serenario. Meanwhile the furnishings in the gallery have been supplemented by pieces bearing the hallmark of furniture from a royal palace. This is the Baroque of Garibaldi's days whereby the nineteenth century decreed that Louis XV was the only style befitting ruling dynasties, from Palazzo dei Normanni to Buckingham Palace and even Bangkok.

Like every other house where people lived, major changes were made in the second half of the nineteenth century when the attractions of public receptions were exchanged for the pleasures of intimacy. Then the homes were converted again to provide English-style rooms, which, in turn, were filled with Second Empire objects imported from Napoleon III's Paris.

A shift to Neoclassical

An exception to the rule of the parameters of the building brief changing during construction and completion phases is provided by Villa Paternò in Spedalotto. The house is entirely in the Neoclassical style and both furnishings and decor are still intact. These are best encapsulated in the main room which is dedicated to cameo portraits lining the walls from the barrel-vaulted ceiling down. Even the number of pieces of furniture in the room seems precisely calculated, there being no place for anything else. Construction of the villa started in 1783 at the start of another style which was to find its guiding spirit in Venanzio Marvuglia. The architect's long life (1729–1814) mirrored the sweeping changes in taste that were to turn Palermo from a hotbed of rocaille into an experimental centre of the Neoclassical and the Gothic revival. Marvuglia's early work included Palazzo Coglitore, Palazzo Costantino and Palazzo Geraci. These buildings were fairly severe and difficult to tell apart from others constructed in the same period by Nicolò Palma and Andrea Gigante. The professional quality of these works nevertheless stands out among the modest Vanvitelli-inspired architecture of the period. This can be seen at Villa Ajroldi, in the seaward prospect of Palazzo Lanza Tomasi in the Foro Italico, or in the Ventimiglia family villa on Corso Calatafimi. His masterly use of stone is even more noticeable in Palazzo Riso and Palazzo Galati. But above all we can admire his work at Villa Villarosa in Bagheria which, together with Villa Inguaggiato in Gigante, constitute the finest examples of Sicilian architectural homage to the highly successful stone-built French châteaux constructed during the reigns of Louis XV and XVI. Working alongside Léon Dufourny, who designed the Neo-classical pavilions in the Botanical Garden, and his own son Emanuele, Marvuglia built Villa Belmonte all'Acquasanta at the end of his career. Here he showed a rigorous regard for Empire style while still maintaining the residential model of the

eighteenth-century Sicilian pleasure palace. Indeed it was Villa Belmonte that triggered the taste for antiquities in Sicily. This was an important trend that was to have a major effect on the work of Giovan Battista Basile and Giuseppe Patricolo, judging from paintings in the National Gallery of Sicily that show scenes of everyday life from the period. The taste for things antique reveals that Sicily was particularly receptive to European trends of the time and it makes Marvuglia the first Sicilian to be aware of the taste for revival.

This aspect of Marvuglia's career is particularly pronounced in the Palazzina Cinese. Here influences from the Chinese fashion in England meld with those of the porcelain factories in Portici and Buen Retiro which produced objects for the Bourbons. Yet, the entire palace is imbued with an extraordinary sense of creativity that was the true strength of early eclecticism. Around any given theme something new could be created. This, in turn, meant that the traditional craft ways of doing things were continually being updated, leading to the climax of Ernesto Basile's brand of Art Nouveau.

Eighteenth-century houses in eastern Sicily

Architecturally speaking, what happened in eastern Sicily during the eighteenth century was very different to events in and around Palermo. The reason for this was the introduction of a unitary plan for the area following the disastrous earthquake in 1693. This resulted in the common stylistic thread being far stronger in the Val di Noto than elsewhere, even though many buildings started in the early years of the eighteenth century were only completed during the following century. Indeed, a number were never completed at all. They were still unfinished when the old regime imploded in the aftermath of the socio-economic changes that followed the unification of Italy. Furniture from the Baroque period in Catania, Noto, Syracuse and Caltanisetta is harder to find than Baroque furniture from Palermo or Trapani, towns that boasted a centuries-long craft tradition. Houses that were properly finished and which their owners used as part of their social life are few and far between. Even then, in some cases, they were not fully constructed until midway through the nineteenth century. Another influencing factor was the Napoleonic Wars. Although Sicily was occupied by the English and became the main allied base in the Mediterranean, the wars still had an effect on the way homes gradually changed. The resulting trend was towards houses emphasizing the quality of life for those who lived in them and away from their official purposes as a place to receive guests, a tendency already discernible at the close of the eighteenth century. In practical terms it can be illustrated by the numerous villas scattered on the outskirts of Palermo and other smaller centres. However, a middle class was beginning to emerge, mainly as a result of the trading opportunities offered by the presence of the British army and navy. This commerce led to the founding of a number of capitalist fortunes. Their possessors were then influenced by tastes and trends in the metropolitan cities of Europe. The Sicily of palaces and castles, which had lasted for so many centuries, now ceased to exist.

Catania

Palazzo Biscari in Catania stands out in the history of the Val di Noto. Its existence is due primarily to Prince Ignazio Paternò di Biscari who wanted his palace to be unique among homes of the Sicilian Enlightenment. In the latter part of the eighteenth century, travelers pursuing the myth of Classical Greece began to include Sicily in the Grand Tour of Italy. They all stopped off at Palazzo Biscari to visit the *antiquarium*. Without a doubt, the prince had no inkling that his rocaille taste was famous throughout Europe for being totally out of touch with the times. So the foreigners poured in having read Winckelmann from cover to cover only to be greeted by a building site for a mansion in a style that Fischer von Erlach had adopted for the homes of German princes some thirty years earlier. Such an undertaking, therefore, could only inspire revulsion in sophisticated travelers. On the other hand, we should remember that as early as 1760 Giambattista Tiepolo had been summoned to Charles III's court in Madrid, where he was promptly passed over in favour of Anton Raphael Mengs. The degree of old-fashioned taste at Palazzo Biscari, the largest house included in the rebuilding of Catania, seems even more provincial when we think of Vanvitelli's design for the Reggia in Caserta. This royal palace, finished in 1774, was the most important monument in a new style fashionable throughout southern Italy. It was in the 1770s that, over at Palazzo Biscari, the finishing touches were being made to the decorations in the ballroom. The reason behind all this lay not merely in the instructions of the client, but also in the pool of craftsmen who were employed to rebuild the Val di Noto after the earthquake. Before the architect Giovan Battista Vaccarini arrived in Catania in 1730, most architects working in the area had been stonemasons in Messina. They included the Amato, Blundo, Viola and Favetta families, who inclined more to decoration than pure architecture. Not for them the study of treatises on the subject or the seventeenth-century love of planning and creating environments from opposing tensions, which was the hallmark of the great architecture of the day. They preferred to clad simple surfaces in stone, using the fruits of Mannerism as their model. They revived embossment and monsters as favoured by Calamech in Messina a century and a half earlier. It is this type of craft-based architecture that played the most important role in rebuilding the Val di Noto. This frenzy seemed to reverberate throughout the whole of eastern Sicily, unleashing bizarre fantasies from Catania to Ragusa, Syracuse, Noto and Scicli. In Catania its triumph was the east façade of the Benedictine monastery of San Nicola l'Arena. Tuscan Mannerism was originally derived from Michelangelo with figures contorting with the urgency of revolt, as can be seen in depictions of the *prisons* or *Judgment* painted by the master's early disciples. By the eighteenth century, however, this was reduced in the Val di Noto to fantastical ornamentation.

Nonetheless, the few remaining eighteenth-century interiors that have survived in eastern Sicily, and especially those in Palazzo Biscari, did escape the repetitiveness that occurred in some studios. Indeed, the continuous use of ornamentation in these decorative schemes seems a deliberate attempt to recapture the great international period of decorative rocaille. Craftsmen from different studios appear to have been guided by a single mind, which must have been aware of the major models of this culture across Europe, from Venice to the German principalities.

Noto and Syracuse

Like Catania, the plans for reconstructing Noto were drawn up by the government. Here, however, they were implemented by architects who were fully abreast of what was happening in the very best residential building projects across Europe. Even today, visitors are still astounded by the homogeneity of the buildings, by the way the town serves as the administrative centre of ecclesiastical and baronial power, and by the coherence of the plan, which does not distinguish between religious and civil architecture. Everything here contributes to the sense of harmony of a centre which governed possessions four times greater than the territory under its direct control. The Duca di Camastra appointed Carlos De Grunembergh, a Dutch military engineer working for the Spanish crown, to oversee reconstruction. Camastra and De Grunembergh's project did not stop at town planning but, more importantly, laid down a series of economic incentives attached to the expropriation and re-assignment of land. It was this that encouraged the financially powerful feudal landowners, barons and clergy to get involved. It also opened the way for a true urban development plan to be introduced. This in turn was the force that pushed reconstruction forward for over a hundred years. In 1866, church land was confiscated and the bureaucratic role that the viceroyal government had given to Noto suddenly ceased to exist. Almost overnight, the town's prosperity evaporated. But the unique quality and homogeneity of this singular urban development in Sicily under Spanish rule makes Noto of paramount interest to European conservationists.

Most of Noto's palazzi were built in the second half of the eighteenth century. They followed guidelines drawn up by Grunembergh and by other architects such as local mathematician Giovanni Battista Landolina Salonia and the Jesuit priest Angelo Italia. But the true architects of the remarkable outcome were Rosario Gagliardi, Paolo Labisi and Vincenzo Sinatra. The town unfolds on either side of a main axis provided by Corso Vittorio Emanuele off which three large piazze lead. All the monumental ecclesiastical buildings are found along this route. On the intersecting streets leading to the Upper Town lie the palazzi belonging to the baronial families of Trigona di Canicarao, Astuto and Villadorata. The palazzi, decorated on the

cusp of the eighteenth and nineteenth centuries, contain quadrature and paintings by various local artists. Their work marks the arrival in the provinces of the figurative fashion triggered by the rediscovery of the remains of Herculaneum. In Sicily, this fashion directly replaced Empire Style and continued into the middle of the nineteenth century when it was overtaken by Romanticism. It was almost as if connections to the centre were extremely weak and models from the past were degraded to the point of being little more than the type of art found in popular oleographs. Because they were either replaced or changed, nearly all of the furniture and furnishings found in eastern Sicily are nineteenth century, mainly of the Umbertine style beloved of the lesser aristocracy and middle classes who knew little of what was happening in France or the world beyond. This pseudo-palazzo style was to spread into the smaller villas in Palermo. These were owned by country barons who moved into the Via Libertà area of the city at the close of the nineteenth century.

In Syracuse too, the reconstruction of the Val di Noto produced projects of great cultural value. The best example is Piazza del Duomo. As soon as one enters the piazza one is able to see Palazzo Beneventano del Bosco, an extraordinary example of how rocaille survived right up to the dawn of the new century. It was built on a site that had previously housed a medieval building which, in the seventeenth century, had been the seat of the Knights of Malta. Luciano Alì, an architect from Syracuse who had evidently kept abreast of trends in France and Naples, reconstructed the entire side which faces onto the piazza. Although he added a large tribune, his masterpiece was to introduce a staircase between the two courtyards, reminiscent of the one built by Andrea Gigante thirty years earlier at Palazzo Bonagia in Palermo. The courtyard still has its original cobblestones with their Louis XVI ornamental patterns. It is almost as if it were Sicily's farewell to the European model.

Revivals in Palermo in the early nineteenth century

Innovations in the design field reached Palermo more quickly than elsewhere on the island. Therefore, it was in the capital that the fashion for revivals permeated everything that its craftsmen produced, from bookcases to brass bedsteads and silverware. All their work shows signs of the growing appetite for items in the style of Louis Philippe. It should be remembered that contacts with England, Sicily's protecting power, were close. On the other hand, its ties with France continued to be strong. The fact was that Louis Philippe spent many years as an exile in Palermo waiting for the political climate in France to favour his return home.

At the dawn of the new century, Palermo was already a very international city. The lay culture produced works of considerable value. During the long reign of Ferdinand IV, it was thanks to the Bourbon officials, particularly the Duca Di Serradifialco, that the new interest in archeological remains did not turn into their wholesale disposal on the antiques market, as happened in Greece and Asia Minor.

Palermo in the nineteenth century

In Palermo more than anywhere else in Sicily, the illusion of a happy transition to the long-awaited reunion with mainstream Europe was to produce a vital period in the newly international city's history. The fact that France and England now governed the Mediterranean countries of North Africa elevated Palermo to the rank of crossroads for European commercial interests. The city saw itself as the emporium of the east. At the start of the twentieth century, every palazzo in Palermo boasted photographs signed by the royal guests who had stayed there. Foremost among these were the Prussian rulers Edward IV and William II. During this period, the kaisers rekindled memories of their descent from the Hohenstaufen emperors of the past and set out to reconquer an area of influence in the eastern Mediterranean, from which Germany had been excluded since Manfred died at Benevento. Under the guise of social niceties, what we are really seeing is the prelude to the First World War. The ephemeral nature of the prosperity had, in fact, already

been sensed by the great trading families that had settled in Palermo during the nineteenth century. By the time the Great War began, the English dynasties that had made their fortunes from general commerce and, in particular, the export of fortified Marsala wines, had already practically pulled out of the island. Of the various branches of the Whitaker clan, the only one to stay in Sicily was Joseph Isaac's family and this was because Isaac was actually more interested in archeology than in finance.

The period at the turn of this century is still remembered by the inhabitants of Palermo as a golden age. It was a time of happiness imprinted in the collective memory which has only recently begun to revisit its unique artistic heritage. Indeed, the period did possess all the hallmarks of a golden age: a plan shared rather than acted on, an idea of happiness that all could recognize, a thought that could sustain morale during years of delusion. There is no question that this notion was based on exceptionally good economic circumstances. However, even by the end of the nineteenth century, it was evident that these circumstances had already ceased to exist.

At the start of the twentieth century, the mainstay of this illusion was the Florio family. The image was buoyed up by a regal stream of spending, by a liberality that shifted from production to paternalism (at a time when in Europe the Industrial Revolution had produced great hardship in the labour market). This shift was underpinned by huge amounts of financial capital as well as enormous sums spent on entertaining at receptions and functions. All this combined to inject an image of financial solidity into the first twenty years of the new century. The Florio and Whitaker family homes symbolize taste in Palermo during the second half of the nineteenth century. In the eclecticism of the buildings, the taste of the day reflects a whole range of contradictions found in Palermo society itself at the close of the century. A common feature is the growth in spending which, in itself, mirrors the shift from a feudal society to one in contact with international trade and the fashion for collecting.

Originally the Baroque palazzi had a discreetly minimal amount of furniture. Just a few consoles, divans and armchairs would be lined up along the walls. During the course of the nineteenth century, however, they started to fill up with upholstered furniture and all manner of collections, particularly porcelain.

Knick-knacks invaded every corner while fashion and furniture reviews guided the taste of the buyers. This was especially true of those who ventured to the cities of their dreams. No longer content with just visiting Naples, people now went further afield to London, Paris, Vienna, Munich and Amsterdam. Resembling giant jewel cases, the palazzi of Palermo began to fill with souvenirs. For years thereafter the remains of the city's glory fuelled the antiques trade which sold furniture made in Palermo alongside that from Genoa and Piedmont. For their part, middle-class clients delighted in the thought that they were stimulating the creative juices of local design. There were conflicting trends vying for control of the role of the home and of the house as a status symbol. On the one hand, there was still a certain kind of social life that was based on the clan. At the other extreme, a new society was emerging based on smaller groups who enjoyed the same places, entertainment and travel.

Then, one of those rare moments took place where design meets its middle-class clients in a fertile environment. It happened in late nineteenth-century Palermo, which was then host to the 1892 Exhibition. Milan was also to experience such a moment between 1935 and 1975. In Sicily it was Ernesto Basile's moment. Basile was a master of eclecticism. He promoted a range of ideas from the Renaissance revival of his design for Villa Bordonaro in the Croci district to originating the fashion for Art Nouveau architecture in his work on Vincenzo Florio's villino in Olivuzza. The foreign merchants, on the other hand, clung to different, orthodox tastes. When they commissioned houses, they did not choose their architects from among the leaders of the local revival. Rather, they looked for inspiration to Norman medieval castles or used Carnilivari as their model. The Whitakers called in Henry Christian to build their Gothic mansion on Via Cavour and, when they commissioned Ignazio Greco to design Villa Malfitano, they made him copy the Tuscan Renaissance revival Villa Favard on Lungarno Vespucci. Ernesto Basile was only ever allowed to refurbish the interior of Villa Sofia, the third residence of this dynastic family. Meanwhile, in Taormina, the English designer Robert Hawthorn Kitson brought in the ideas of the Arts and Crafts Movement, importing them wholesale into a villa and garden that he called Casa Cuseni. Inspired by the unquenchable British taste for all things Palladian,

in 1908–10 he called in Frank Brangwyn, a member of William Morris's circle, to decorate the dining room. The two rooms Brangwyn decorated are listed as national treasures in the register kept at the Victoria and Albert Museum.

Homes, architecture and design in the twentieth century

The change in the social role played by the home as a status symbol and the new ambitions of the international bourgeoisie, who did not see the need to have showcase homes bolstering their own prestige, were reflected in the fact that Ernesto Basile was never commissioned to build a mansion for any of the new financial dynasties of Palermo. Working closely with the Ducrot furniture factory, his real sphere of influence lay in the designs he produced for the middle classes of Palermo at the turn of the century. This influence lasted right up to the time when it was superseded by Italian Bauhaus in the 1930s. Until then the model bourgeois house in Palermo looked to Basile for its design ideas. In addition to this, various other proponents of the Art Nouveau floral style were also influenced by him, as can be seen in Filippo La Porta's Villino Caruso and those built by both Ernesto Armò and Salvatore Caronia Roberti before the First World War. The flourishing atmosphere in turn-of-the-century Palermo was fed by the emergence of an urban middle class, the first time it had ever been seen in the city and whose return has been awaited ever since. A different matter was the lower middle class which worked for the political administration and which still holds so much power in the island's capital. These were people who had arrived in Palermo during the first twenty years of the *Statuto Speciale Siciliano*, swelling the population by 400,000. Their taste was for the mass-produced neo-Baroque furniture that Barraja turned out, for wrought-iron gates and multi-coloured Murano glass with a gilt finish. So, by the time the Second World War was over, little was left to indicate the survival of a once great cultural tradition. Among private houses, probably only Giuseppe Samonà's Villino Scimemi can be held up as an example. It reminds us that over the centuries Palermo has been a meeting place of architects and artists, a place where creativity, design and architecture flourished, a city in the vanguard of the quest for a better quality of life.

Palazzi of Sicily

The Salone della Minerva (Hall of Minerva) of Palazzo Mazzarino in Palermo.

Palazzo Reale in Palermo

It is generally accepted that the Arabs began the construction of what was later to be the residence of the Norman kings, Palazzo Reale, on the site of Paleapoli – the fortified city that had been founded by the Carthaginians possibly earlier than the seventh century and destined to become the inner part of "Panormos". Tommaso Fazello, in his *De rebus siculis decades duae* (Twenty Years of Sicilian History), of 1558, noted the existence of a number of engraved letters inside the palace. According to these, it was "built by the Saracens on the ruins of an ancient fortress, shortly after they had conquered Palermo." Moreover, remains from the Arab period may be found beneath the Cappella Palatina (Palatine Chapel), in the crypt and other subterranean areas.

The existence of an "ancient fortress" in the pre-Arab period has recently been confirmed by the discovery of a section of Punic wall, dating from the fifth century BC, under the sixteenth-century part of the palace. However, the assertion made by the nineteenth-century scholar Salvatore Morso, that the "supreme authority" had its seat here not only under the

Above
Palazzo Reale, in a watercolor plate from *Teatro geografico antiguo y moderno del Reyno de Sicilia*, Madrid, Biblioteca Nazionale, 1686.

Opposite
A view of Palazzo Reale, with the monument of Philip V, erected in 1661 by the sculptor Carlo d'Aprile, in the foreground. The original bronze statue was replaced in the nineteenth century with a marble sculpture by Nunzio Morello.

Carthaginians and the Arabs but also in the intervening period under the Romans and the Goths, remains open to question. If a *Qasr* ("castle" in Arabic) did exist in the Arab period on the site of the present-day palace, it was certainly not the only fortified complex in the city at that time; nor did it serve continuously as the residence of the emir. About a century after the conquest of Sicily by the Muslims, who established the capital of the island at Palermo, the displacement of the Aghlabite dynasty by the Fatimites led to a destabilizing of political power. To set up a defense against possible invasion from the sea, as well as the hostility of part of the civilian population itself, the emirs were compelled in 937-938 to move the center of power away from old Paleapoli and build a new fortified citadel, named *al-Halisah* ("the Chosen"), close to the coast. By the time of the Norman conquest of Sicily, which began in 1061, *Balàrmuh*, the Arabic transliteration of the Greek *Panormos*, which means "all port," was one of the richest and most thriving cities in the Mediterranean, fully part of the great civilization of the Islamic world.

In a vast treatise on all the countries known at that time, which was completed in 1154 and dedicated to Roger II, the Arab geographer al-Idrisi described the capital in tones of wonder: "Balarm, the vast and beautiful city; the great and splendid place; the most

precious and exceptional city in the world ... Palermo has buildings of such beauty that travelers make their way here [drawn] by reports of the [marvels of the] architecture." Among these buildings the royal residence was of course pre-eminent.

On the highest part of the Cassaro, the formidable King Roger had his new citadel made from small pieces of mosaic stone and large blocks of freestone, following the rules of art, furnished with high towers reinforced with lookouts and ramparts, and containing houses and well-built halls. It is notable for its architectural decoration, for its rare and marvelous calligraphic ornament, and for the variety of elegant figures to be found there.

One of the earliest known sources of information about Palazzo Reale, the account by al-Idrisi, describes a monumental complex which has since been completely transformed by time and history, and which retains only a few fragments of its Norman origins, significant as they may be. Al-Idrisi implied that Roger II, the first Norman king, was responsible for the commencement of the building, or at least for the radical transformation of an earlier building into a "New Palace". It was splendidly "arranged, decorated, and in every sense designed for refined living," according to a source of some decades later, Ugo Falcando, a historian at the Norman court (c.1190). Falcando records that the

palace was "surrounded by a great circular wall."

Located at the edge of the city on the side away from the sea, and consisting of an irregular polygonal courtyard with a tower at each corner, the palace stood as a defense against the mountains and opened its gates onto the city. By comparing Falcando's exhaustive description with what remains today of the residence of the Altavilla family, it is possible to identify the various parts of the original Norman structure and to establish the function of each.

The tower on the right (looking at the palace from the city), part of which still stands, is known as the Torre Pisana, or Torre di Santa Ninfa. According to Falcando, it served as a treasury, and, indeed, the lower of the rooms on the two upper levels has been identified as the treasury and mint. The upper floor, which must have held the throne room, consists of a square central room twice the height of those on either side and covered with cross-vaulting. Some fragments of a mosaic depicting battle scenes – possibly the valiant military exploits of the Altavilla family – were discovered when the Norman rooms were renovated.

The residential aspect of the Norman building is apparent in a number of better preserved rooms in the wing which has partly survived, next to the Torre Pisana: the Gioaria, from the Arabic al-

gawariyah, which means "the shining." In the small portion that remains of the residential area of the palace, there are a number of rooms that are markedly Arab in design: the Sala degli Armigeri (Hall of the Armigers), the Stanza di Re Ruggero (Hall of King Roger), and the Sala delle Quattro Colonne (Hall of the Four Columns), later known as the Sala dei Venti (Hall of the Winds). The last of these consists of a square room, the central part of which is now covered by a wooden ceiling, not original, which rests by means of pointed arches on four stone columns.

Next to the Sala delle Quattro Colonne is the magnificent Stanza di Re Ruggero (Hall of King Roger). Its mosaics date from a period spanning the reign of William I and that of William II (1160–1170), except the vault, which dates from the time of Frederick II and has the Hohenstaufen eagle in its centre, and several other areas which were subjected to heavy restoration work in the last century. The mosaic decoration covers the upper part of the walls, and includes a *Hunting Scene*, a *Battle of Centaurs*, and *Animals Facing Each Other* across trees and palms – leopards, peacocks, deer, and swans – all silhouetted against a gold background.

The mosaic decoration of the Stanza di Re Ruggero, the fragments of the Torre Pisana, and the mosaics in the Sala della Fontana (Hall of the Fountain) of the Castello della Zisa have generally

Below
The Stanza di re Ruggero (Hall of King Roger) in the Gioaria. In the foreground, a very precious table, its top made from a petrified tree trunk. Originally part of the Bourbon furnishings of the Villa Favorita in Portici.

Opposite
One of the mosaic lunettes of the Stanza di Re Ruggero, showing, in the lower panel, *Two Leopards Facing Each Other, Flanked by Two Peacocks*, and, above, a *Battle of Centaurs*. The vault has been dated to the period of Frederick.

been attributed to Byzantine artists, though it has yet to be established to what extent secular mosaic decoration in the Norman period was influenced by Islamic culture, the iconographic contribution of which is clear. Indeed, the relationship between the architectural elements and building techniques of the rooms of the Torre Pisana and the Gioaria and certain examples of Muslim architecture, particularly from the Fatimite period, is unmistakable.

Falcando devotes some time to the Cappella Palatina, also called the Cappella di S. Pietro. Entering the palace from the city side, you come first of all to the Royal Chapel, its floor magnificently worked, the lower part of the walls decorated with slabs of precious marble and the upper part with pieces of mosaic, some gold, some colored, which depict the stories of the Old and New Testaments. The lofty wood ceiling is distinguished by the elegance of the carving, by the wonderful variety of the painting, and by the dazzling splendor of the gold. The chapel, a unique masterpiece, predates the Stanza di re Ruggero and the rooms of the Torre Pisana. Built by Roger II in 1131, a year after he was crowned king of Sicily, this little church was consecrated in 1140. The product of a fusion of the longitudinal Latin three-nave plan and the central Byzantine one, the church combines elements that unmistakably are Islamic

in origin (the pointed arches supporting the columns of the nave, the magnificent alveolar wooden ceiling painted with secular images) with a rich mosaic decoration similar to slightly earlier models from Constantinople and Russia. The effect culminates in the powerful image

of *Christ Pantocrator* in the dome of the apse.

Little is known of the evolution of the palace in the Hohenstaufen, Angevin, and Aragonese periods. It is likely that these centuries saw the strengthening of the castle's fortifications, since alterations made in the sixteenth century

included the destruction of numerous towers.

At the end of the fourteenth century the palace of the Norman monarchs was abandoned. The royal seat was transferred first to the *Hosterium Magnum* (Great Hall), a house seized from the Chiaramonte family in 1392, and then, in the early years of the sixteenth century, to the Castello a Mare. For a while the Norman palace became the seat of the Inquisition, during which time it fell into a ruinous state. A complex scheme of coastal fortification, intended to form a defense against pirate raids and the expansion of the Turkish naval forces, came to involve the construction of the fortified Spanish walls of Palermo, which included the rampart of S. Pietro situated behind the palace. It was in the wake of these developments that, in 1553, the viceroy Giovanni de Vega decided to re-establish the seat of power in the historic palace of the kings of Sicily. The medieval buildings were renovated and a number of new wings built. In the second half of the sixteenth century, there were a great many Italian and Flemish artists working at Palazzo Reale, artists who came in the retinue of the viceroys, bringing with them a late Mannerist style.

The Cremonese painter Giovanni Paolo Fonduli arrived in Palermo in 1568 in the retinue of Ferdinando de Avalos, Marchese di Pescara. None of his work remains but he became the leading artist in a workshop established during the 1570s by the viceroy, the Marchese di Terranova, together with the Fleming Simon de Wobreck and the Sicilian Giuseppe Alvino. The same "team" continued to be active during the viceroyship of Marcantonio Colonna, who had returned victorious from Lepanto, and who, according to the testimony of the Marchese di Villabianca, "then enlarged [the palace] with additional apartments in 1583 ..." Fonduli and Alvino – the latter the principal artist on this occasion – decorated various rooms with canvases and frescoes, which alternated with stuccowork characterized by curvilinear motifs. The same period saw the construction of three of the four sides of the smaller of the palace's two courtyards, the Cortile della Fontana (Courtyard of the Fountain), square and pensile, with a gallery on two sides at ground level and perhaps one on all four sides of the upper storey. It would seem that part of it was built during the viceroyship of Marcantonio Colonna – more precisely, in the early 1580s, during which time the Tuscan Camillo Camilliani might have worked there.

The alterations during the sixteenth-century extended also to the formal reception area of the palace. The 1560s and 1570s saw the erection of a new three-storey wing, the outer walls of which overlook the city (the plain of S. Teresa). For this to take place, a number of medieval

buildings had to be demolished, including the external wall of the Norman castle. The façade looking onto the countryside, was left rough and fortified, and was given a neo-medieval covering in the nineteenth century.

The upper floor of the new wing housed the Sala Grande dei Parlamenti Generali (Great Hall of the General Parliaments), which, according to the Marchese di Villabianca, "was built by Giovanni la Cerda, the Duca di Medinaceli, in 1560, and brought to perfection a decade later by the viceroy the Marchese di Pescara Avalos." Transformed in the nineteenth century into the Sala d'Ercole (Hall of Hercules), it appears, in what must be almost its original state, in a watercolor of 1686 in the *Teatro geografico antiguo y moderno del Reyno di Sicilia* (Ancient and Modern Geographical Theatre of the Kingdom of Sicily), and in a fresco by Gerardo Astorino in one of the Sale del Duca di Montalto (Halls of the Duke of Montalto) on the first floor of the new wing. Also known as the Sale delle Udienze Estive (Halls of the Summer Audiences), these rooms were created by Don Luigi Moncada, Duca di Montalto, the viceroy's deputy, out of what was formerly a munitions deposit. In 1636 Moncada assigned the decoration of the rooms (little of which has survived to the present day) to four of the leading painters of the time – Vincenzo la Barbera, Giuseppe Costantino, Gerardo Astorino, and Pietro Novelli.

The first radical alterations, however, were made during the viceroyship of Bernardino Cardines, Duca di Maqueda (1598–1601), and include the construction of both the Cortile Maqueda (Maqueda Courtyard) – square, with galleries on three levels – and of the wing

facing the city. Work on the second floor of the latter had in fact commenced a little after the middle of the sixteenth century; it still retains its main entrance and four rustic windows. The exterior of the next three floors, which were divided by strong horizontal cornices, has been preserved almost intact, the principal floor showing a classical arrangement of windows, in which triangular and curved tympanums alternate. The appearance of the palace had thus

El Virrey

EL Capᵗ dela Guardia

EL Protonotario

EL Secretᵗⁱᵒ de Guerra

Las Porteras deCamara

10

El Sacro Conʃⁱᵒ

EL Brazo Ecleſiaſtᶜᵒ

EL Brazo Militar

EL Brazo Demanial

La Virreyna y Las
Damaſ

10

EL PAR   LA   MENTO

changed significantly on the side facing the city, the side on which the piazza was built.

The interior of the new wing was used for social gatherings, with the Galleria taking up much of the principal floor. At the instigation of the viceroy Benavides, Conte di S. Stefano, and according to some with the assistance of the architect Paolo Amato, the Galleria was decorated in 1682 with maps of Malta and Sicily, and, as the Marchese di Villabianca records, with "pictures of the kings of Sicily, to match those of their representatives, the viceroys, which adorned the antechambers ..." The original appearance of this room, which was later altered and to which today's Sala Gialla (Yellow Hall) roughly corresponds, is recorded in a watercolor in the the abovementioned *Teatro geografico antiguo y moderno del Reyno di Sicilia*, of 1686. Villabianca continues: "The portraits of the same princes that may be seen there today were renovated in 1738 by His Majesty Charles Bourbon, King of Sicily, now glorious monarch of Spain, who assigned the work to the excellent painter Guglielmo Borremans ...; the same period saw, again at Charles's instigation, the construction of the superb royal staircase, in red stone, which is truly magnificent."

These works initiated a new and intensive phase of architectural and decorative modification, which began at the time of the coronation of

Charles III in Palermo in 1735 and continued throughout the reign of Ferdinand III (1759–1825), particularly in the two periods in which the Bourbon court was resident at Palermo (1798–1802 and 1806–1815). The decoration of the Sala del Parlamento, by the Sicilian Giuseppe Velasco

and the Neapolitan ornamentalist Benedetto Cotardi, dates from 1811–1812. The room, which from that time served as the reception room of the Bourbon court, came to be called the Sala d'Ercole, after the paintings on the ceiling and the walls. The *Apotheosis* and the *Labours* of scenes (an obvious reference to the decoration of the columns in the Logge di Raffaello in the Vatican, which were widely known through engravings).

The decoration of a number of other rooms also dates from the nineteenth century. Around 1830, the

the mythological hero Hercules, the latter painted in monochrome, were arranged between bands of grotesque decoration and garlands that are neoclassical and neo-Raphaelesque in style, interrupted by monochromatic Galleria was transformed into the Sala Gialla, the ceiling decorated with the *Stories of Count Roger Conquering Palermo* by Vincenzo Riolo, Giovanni Patricolo and Giuseppe Patania. In the same period Patania painted the ceiling of

Above
The monochrome depiction of *Hercules on the Pyre* is painted on the walls of the hall.

Opposite
Two of the labours of Hercules painted on the walls of the hall – *Hercules and Cerberus* and *Hercules and Cacus*.

the Stanza delle Dame (Room of the Ladies), also known as the Stanza della Regina (Room of the Queen), using a repertoire of images inspired by the works of Raphael in the Vatican and of decorative motifs borrowed from the engravings in the *Antichità di Ercolano* (*Antiquities of Herculaneum*) which were to become so fashionable in Palermo in the second half of the nineteenth century. The Sala da Pranzo (Dining Hall) was decorated by Giovanni Patricolo in Chinese style, inspired by the scenes painted by Velasco in the Palazzina Cinese a few decades earlier. The decoration of a number of rooms with allegorical and mythological themes and ornamental plant and flower motifs dates from the second half of the nineteenth century, a phase that ended in 1901 with Salvatore Gregorietti's work on the present-day Sala dei Viceré (Hall of the Viceroys). Since 1947 Palazzo Reale has been the seat of the Sicilian Regional Assembly, which has promoted a series of works dedicated to the recovery of the building's underlying Norman structures.

Opposite
The Stanza della Regina (Room of the Queen) was decorated by Giuseppe Patania around 1830.

Below
A detail of the decoration of the Sala Cinese (Chinese Hall), which was painted with oriental scenes by Giovanni Patricolo in the nineteenth century.

La Zisa in Palermo

In 1154 the Arab geographer al-Idrisi wrote as follows: "On all sides of the capital of Sicily [the land] is furrowed by water and broken up by perennial springs. Palermo is rich in fruit; its buildings and its places of delight confound those who attempt to describe them and dazzle the intellect. In short, anyone who looks at this city will soon find his head spinning."

The hunting grounds and pleasure gardens which, in accordance with Muslim custom, surrounded Palermo at one time contained residential buildings and were strewn with pavilions and fountains. Contemporaries described them in tones of wonder. Today, only a few fragments remain; the Castello di Maredolce is the most ancient of these and is of Arab origin, while La Cuba Sottana and La Cuba Soprana, La Zisa, and perhaps the Castello dello Scribene, were built by the Norman kings. The latter group may nevertheless be regarded as belonging to Islamic culture, not only on account of their architectural style, but more particularly in view of the type of residence they represent: the royal retreat, intended for periods of rest

Above
La Zisa, in an anonymous painting of 1831 (private collection).

Opposite
The main façade of La Zisa, one of the numerous royal retreats which, in the words of Ibn Gubayr, an Arab traveller from Valencia who passed through Sicily in 1185, encircled "the throat of the city as a necklace encircles the neck of a full-bosomed young woman."

and holidays, set in exuberant gardens and surrounded by fishponds, artificial lakes and elaborate water systems – a re-creation of the paradise described in the Koran.

The best preserved of the royal retreats is La Zisa, its name deriving from the Arabic *al-Aziz*, which means "the splendid". It was built for William I. The historian Ugo Falcando (c.1190) wrote that "William decided that just as his father had built La Favara, Il Minenio and other pleasure palaces, so he would build a palace which in its comfort and artistic perfection would surpass those of his father." And he succeeded, but for the fact that, as Falcando went on, "having erected most of the palace, with astonishing speed and at great expense, he was struck down by dysentery before bringing it to perfection, and slowly began to fade away."

This was in 1166. William died, leaving the throne to his son, William II, to whom the final stages of the project, including the decoration, may therefore be attributed.

The paradise-garden that surrounded La Zisa, now completely overrun by urban expansion, at one time made its way into the first floor of the royal residence, flowing through the entrance hall into the Sala della Fontana (Hall of the Fountain), where flora and fauna became art, mingling with mosaic and carved stone.

A stream of water which gushed from a fountain at the back of the room came flowing over a tilted slab of marble carved with a zigzag pattern.

According to a description of 1526 by the Bolognese friar Leandro Alberti, it ran throughout the entire room, flowing through "an artificial rill of white marble" and pouring into various basins, where, "through the bright, transparent water one could see mosaic fish of various kinds, subtly composed, which seemed to move in the play of the shining water." The water then passed into an underground channel, only to reappear in a large fishpond in front of the palace, which had at its center "a fine and charming building, also square in shape."

La Zisa was provided with thermal baths and its own external chapel, dedicated to the Holy Trinity, with a single nave and a stalactitic vault in the sanctuary. In keeping with the typology of Fatimite residential buildings, the retreat at La Zisa has a strict and compact geometric form, in which two turrets on the short sides, erected to house the ventilation pipes, constitute the only protruding elements. The walls of the building, which are composed of square stone blocks, regularly arranged, originally bore a number of decorative elements: cornices, blind ogival arches, arched lintels, and small windows, some with a single light and some with two, which once opened onto the façade, and which were replaced by large rectangular windows in the seventeenth century. The interior has also

Above and opposite
The coat of arms supported by two lions placed above the central arch of the main façade and the arch itself.

been extensively modified and is characterized by the cross-vaulting typical of north African Fatimite architecture. It has three floors, and consists of a square central area, which was used for reception, and two side wings, in which the private rooms were arranged according to a strictly symmetrical plan.

A fine entrance hall with three arches leads into the Sala della Fontana, which occupies the central part of the ground floor. The Sala is covered with ogival vaulting and is twice the height of the rooms on either side of it, extending up into the second floor. A number of surviving features define the room as a place of reception: the walls, lined with the finest marble edged with strips of mosaic featuring the Islamic motif of the eight-pointed star; the columns, with their finely carved capitals, standing in pairs at the sides of the arches in the entrance hall and softening the edges of the Sala. Also the rich *muqarnas* decoration in the niche above the fountain, in the two side niches, and at one time in the vault of the entrance hall, too; and the magnificent mosaics, depicting, inside three discs, two pairs of *Peacocks Facing Each Other* across palm trees and a pair of *Archers* shooting at birds in a tree.

The Muslim origin of the *muqarnas* that decorate this and many other rooms of La Zisa, creating magical chiaroscuro effects, is unmistakable.

Opinions differ, however, regarding the highly skilled creators of the mosaic depictions. These have been related to the hunting and animal scenes in the Stanza di Ruggero of the Palazzo Reale in Palermo, and also to the *Battle between Two Lions and Two Camels Facing Each Other Across a Palm Tree* embroidered on the famous *Mantle of King*

Roger, now in the Weltliche Schatzkammer in Vienna. The mosaic decoration of La Zisa, traditionally attributed to Byzantine artists, shows that the strong Islamic-Fatimite component of civil buildings constructed during the Norman period also extended into this sphere.

The two wings of the palace, starting from the ground floor, had to follow a strictly symmetrical plan. They contained the two spiral staircases – renovated as part of a twentieth-century restoration project with only partial respect for their original form. These wound around a central pillar, linking one floor to another. There are various rooms in the two wings of the second floor, with small connecting rooms between them. These may have constituted two private apartments, perhaps reserved for the harem, given that the two windows of the respective entrance halls, at one time furnished with grilles, overlooked the Sala della Fontana. This would have allowed the women to observe the social encounters that took place there without being seen. There are two further residential apartments, with a similar distribution of rooms, in the two wings of the third floor of the palace. Finally, there is a spacious roof-terrace, above the covered areas of the third floor.

The custom of *villeggiatura* (holidaying in the country) was revived by the aristocracy from the beginning of the fifteenth century, after two centuries when the area outside Palermo was abandoned as a result of continuous raids by Angevins and Saracens. While a number of Norman suburban residences were given over to religious Orders, others were acquired by patrician families and modernized.

During this period La Zisa underwent a number of alterations, including the destruction of the inscribed frieze crowning the façade, from which the merlons were created, and the opening of two windows on the third floor, one on each side of the central window.

In 1440 La Zisa was granted to the Bolognese poet Antonio Beccadelli, known as "Il Panormita" (The

Below
The lobby of the third floor, which was altered during the works commissioned by the Sandoval family. In the background, the Sala del Belvedere looks onto the main façade through what was once a two-light window.

Opposite
The archway between the entrance hall and the Sala della Fontana (Hall of the Fountain) on the ground floor.

Palermitan). Fifty years later it passed to the viceroy of Acuña, and after that to various families, including the Alliatas, the Spadaforas, the Ventimiglia di Geraci family, and the Oppezingas, until 1635, when it was acquired by Giovanni de Sandoval, who was responsible for the seventeenth-century alterations. The two-light windows were removed and the roof-terrace was extended over the previously uncovered areas of the third floor, while the wall between the central lobby and the Sala del Belvedere was replaced by an arch. The two small staircases were replaced with a single grand staircase. The entrance hall on the first floor was split into two levels, and two new, smaller entrance arches were constructed, one inside the principal arch on the façade and the other inside the entrance to the Sala della Fontana. The two-light windows of the façade were replaced by larger rectangular windows, while new windows were made in the rear and lateral walls. Inside the building, a number of walls were knocked down to create larger rooms. Few changes have been made to the building since the seventeenth century.

La Zisa remained in the hands of the Sandoval family until the beginning of the nineteenth century, when it passed to the Notarbartolo princes of Sciara, who retained possession of the house until it was acquired by the Region of Sicily.

Palazzo Chiaramonte, known as "Lo Steri", in Palermo

Following the revolt against Angevin rule in 1282, the feudal lords of Sicily granted sovereignty to the kings of Aragon, who held a dynastic right to the throne. (Pietro d'Aragona had married the daughter of Manfred Hohenstaufen.) The fourteenth century was, in fact, a period of total anarchy, with the island effectively governed by a number of powerful Sicilian families who were frequently at war among themselves.

The two most powerful noble families in Palermo, the Sclafanis and the Chiaramontes, promoted a series of works that altered the predominantly Arab face of the city. As a statement of baronial power, they erected imposing fortified palaces which, due to their deliberate isolation from their surroundings and highly conspicuous nature, set out to rival the traditional seats of royal and ecclesiastical power.

In 1330 the residence of the Sclafani family was constructed directly opposite Palazzo Reale, while the *domus magna* of the Chiaramonte family in Piazza Marina more than likely dates from the previous decade. The Chiaramonte family had

Above
Piazza Marina and Palazzo Chiaramonte, in an engraving by F. Ciché (eighteenth century).

Opposite
The north-west corner of Palazzo Chiaramonte, with the third floor added in the second half of the fourteenth century.

acquired already notoriety by the time of the Norman and Hohenstaufen kings. Manfredi I, who died in 1321, had taken part in the Vespers uprising against the Angevins and had supported the nomination of Federico d'Aragona as king of Sicily.

According to a notarial document dated 2 February 1306, Giovanni Chiaramonte il Vecchio (the Elder), the brother of Manfredi I, obtained in emphyteusis from the prior of the convent of S. Maria di Ustica and of S. Onofrio "tenimentum unum terrae vacuae" ("one plot of empty land"), with the obligation to drain and improve it. The land was positioned between the city walls, the sea, the Piano della Marina (Coastal Plain), and the public road running from the Porta del Mare (Sea Gate) – one of the four gates of the *Halisah*, the citadel built as the seat of the Arab emirs in 937–938 – to the ruined church of S. Nicolò dei Latini. On the highest part of this piece of land, at the edge of the Piano della Marina, the magnificent Palazzo Chiaramonte was built.

Recent excavations under the first floor of the palace confirm the belief of the nineteenth-century Arabist Salvatore Morso that the Chiaramonte family made use of a "Palace of the First Muslims", when constructing their own residence. Remains from the Arab and possibly the pre-Arab period have been discovered under a number of rooms on the first floor.

It is still uncertain when Palazzo Chiaramonte was built. The historian Tommaso Fazello, in his *De rebus siculis decades duae* (Twenty Years of Sicilian History), published in 1558, testifies to the existence of "a number of large pieces of land, known as the Pianura di Mare, where the houses of Manfredi Chiaramontano, Conte di Motica, were situated, old buildings, erected in 1320, now known as Osterio."

If the erection of the palace is to be attributed, as seems likely, to Giovanni il Vecchio, who lived until 1339, holding several important positions in Palermo and being permanent leaseholder of the land, the Manfredi mentioned by Fazello is almost certainly to be identified with the most able of its owners, Manfredi III. Manfredi was a far more significant figure politically than his predecessors of the same name, having been one of the four *vicari* (regents) who governed Sicily after the death of Frederick III of Aragon (1377) and during the minority of Queen Mary. This is confirmed by the continuation of the above-quoted extract from Fazello, which mentions this same Manfredi again, as the father of the Andrea who was beheaded in 1392.

Analysis of the original structure of the palace provides one of the most complete impressions of fourteenth-century civil architecture in Sicily: from the island Gothic *koiné* that was born from the meeting of

Right
One of the two-light windows of the palace façade, decorated with lavic inlay of floral and geometric motifs.

Islamified local traditions and more recent western influences imported by the Hohenstaufens, to contemporary Arab northwest African and Hispano-Moorish architectural styles.

The palace is square in shape, and would originally have been built on two levels, in accordance with the canons of urban residential architecture in fourteenth-century Sicily. This would have comprised a first floor compact and without any windows, except perhaps for a number of arrow slits, and a second floor, or *piano nobile*, crowned with a typical cornice of staggered ovoli, and having numerous two- and three-light Gothic windows, irregularly placed, and decorated with lavic inlay of floral and geometric motifs, a technique found in Sicilian architecture as early as the Norman period. The third floor, the windows of which are unfinished and lack

decoration, is likely to have been added in the fourteenth century. Its construction was abandoned in the area of the reception room probably in 1392, following events which brought about the end of the house of Chiaramonte with the beheading of Andrea.

It may be assumed that the second phase of construction dates from the same period as the decoration of the ceiling of the Sala Magna (Great Hall) – namely, 1377–1380 – and thus to the period of Manfredi III. This conclusion is drawn because the construction of the third floor would have entailed flattening the roof above the rooms of the second floor, which must originally have been sloping.

The palace was surrounded by a vast garden which no longer exists. This *viridarium*, which is mentioned in documents, accommodated a number of buildings. The external chapel still stands,

dedicated to St. Anthony, patron saint of the family, and built, it seems, at the instigation of Manfredi III. Traces of pointed arches and columns suggest the existence of a porticoed building, perhaps a stable.

In the Chiaramonte period the palace had a number of entrances, two of them main entrances. Traces of one of the latter have been found in the northern wall. The other, in the southern wall, is still in use and leads into an entrance hall. In the lunette above the entrance, on the inner side, a fresco depicts the patron saint of the Chiaramonte family, *St. George Killing the Dragon*, which must have been painted before 1392, when Andrea, the last member of the family to own the palace, died. Crossing the entrance hall, an open doorway leads into the courtyard, around which there are a number of rooms, including a large hall referred to in documents as the "Sala Tirrana". On the ground floor, the colonnade of the courtyard has two pointed arches on each side; these are supported by tufa columns, the capitals of which are decorated with various kinds of plant motifs.

The second-floor gallery which, according to Giuseppe Spatrisano, was added during the works in the latter part of the fourteenth century, has three arches on each side, resting on columns – one of them from the Arab period – with capitals salvaged from elsewhere.

Opinions differ as to whether the windows of the Sala Magna which overlook the courtyard date from the first or the second half of the fourteenth century. In contrast with the windows of the external façades, which are characterized by flat, two-colour decoration, oriental in

Below
A plant-motif capital from the second floor of the inner courtyard. The column is certainly from the Arab period.

style, the decoration of these is carved and protruding. The dominant feature of the exquisite three-light windows

Opposite
The gallery of the inner courtyard. A niche shows the coat of arms of the Chiaramonte family between the two arches of the second floor.

is typical of fourteenth-century Sicilian architecture, though already used in the Norman period – broken sticks arranged in a zigzag pattern, in some places lying parallel with the surface of the wall (over the arches above the window lights), and in others perpendicular to it (along the cornice inside the lintel).

The Sala Magna, or Sala dei Baroni (Hall of the Barons), located on the northern side of the *piano nobile*, is the most characteristic room in the palace, its extraordinary coffered wooden ceiling – the first of its kind – providing a model for private houses in Sicily up to the end of the fifteenth century. Ferdinando Bologna has noted the influence of the ceiling of the Cappella Palatina at Palazzo Reale, together with an awareness – contrary to the point of view maintained by Sicilianists – of the evolution of the form in the contemporary Islamic world, with particular regard to the Hispano-Moorish ceilings of the Alhambra. According to Ferdinando Bologna, the hanging corbel supporting a truss and connecting it to the wall, a motif that was used in Sicily in the Norman period, was a feature of Islamic architecture from as early as the eleventh century and was still in use in Granada in the middle of the fourteenth century. Hanging corbels are to be found in the Sala Magna of Palazzo Chiaramonte, where they retain their traditional alveolar and stalactitic

form, modified in accordance with the lighter and more sinuous Gothic manner.

As two inscriptions record, the ceiling decoration was commissioned between 1377 and 1380 by Manfredi III Chiaramonte. Simone da Corleone, Cecco di Naro, and Pellegrino de Arena da

Palermo, the artists who signed the ceiling as proof of their authorship, made use of an inexhaustible repertoire of geometric and vegetal decorative motifs of various kinds, framing a complex figurative program composed of scenes from mythology, from the Old Testament, and from chivalry. The wooden ceiling of another room, located in the middle of the eastern side

of the palace, is believed to date from the same period. This one is divided into coffers painted with the coats of arms of illustrious Sicilian families, most likely those related to the Chiaramonte family. Finally, the rediscovered Cappella Palatina on the second floor, dedicated to St. George and the Holy Trinity, also dates from the fourteenth century.

At the end of the century, the Aragonese kings managed to take possession of the island. They landed at Trapani in 1392. On 1 June of that year Count Andrea Chiaramonte was beheaded, having been declared disloyal to the king, Martin I, for having conspired with other barons to prevent the king entering the city. Fazello states that "his head was cut off in the Piazza di Mare, just below his houses, his property having been confiscated and his houses assigned to the King, and the Contado of Modica handed over to Bernardo Caprera." The end of the Chiaramonte family signalled the beginning of the palace's steady decline. "Lo Steri" (from *Hosterium* meaning "Hotel", or "Hall", or "Palace"), or *Regius Hospicius* (Royal Palace) – as the palace is called in documents from the first half of the fifteenth century onwards – became the seat of the Courts of Justice, and of regal and vice-regal power. Following the rebellion of the Palermitans against the government of Viceroy Ugo Moncada in 1516, and against that of

Viceroy Ettore Pignatelli, Duca di Monteleone, a year later, it was considered prudent to transfer the viceregal residence to the more secure Castello a Mare. The ground floor of Lo Steri was then used as the Customs Office, which continued to have its seat there until the twentieth

Opposite
The entrance to the room on the third floor, with the coat of arms of the Chiaramonte family at the top of the arch. The door was made by the Venetian architect Carlo Scarpa.

Below
The remains of a pointed-arch window in the second floor gallery.

century. The date of 1517, given for the departure of the viceregal court, is, however, inconsistent with a contract and note of payment to the painter Vincenzo da Pavia, dated 1520, for a *Nativity* to be painted in the *Regius Hospicius* by order of the viceroy, Ettore Pignatelli, Duca di Monteleone. This period also witnessed the transfer to Lo Steri of the Royal High Court, a judiciary body with competence over civil and criminal cases.

The change in the function of Palazzo Chiaramonte, from private house to seat of political and judiciary power, resulted in a series of works – in particular, the insertion of mezzanines so as to make full use of the available space – that significantly modified the original fourteenth-century structure. While in the fifteenth century the chief concern seems to have been ongoing maintenance, a number of documents from the first two decades of the sixteenth century record the presence of artists and artisans. The painter Antonello de Crescenzio, with his assistants, and "Bartholomeo de Serrantonio florentino fabrolignario" ("Bartholomeo de Serrantonio, Florentine woodworker") received payment in 1503 for works to the roof and other services, in relation to the *camera maior* (great hall) of the residence of the viceroy Giovanni La Nuça. The years 1506–1508 saw payments to Crescenzio "et aliorum pictorum qui depingunt unam cameram superiorem in regio hospicio Panormi in qua habitat et dormit illustris dominus prorex" ("and to other painters who are decorating an upper room in the Royal Palace in Palermo, in which the Illustrious Viceroy lives and sleeps"). The viceroy at that time was Raimondo de Cardona, for whom the painter also produced "quadrum unum de tabolis" ("one painted tablet"). Crescenzio, whose name appears in documents in relation to various other decorative works, is generally regarded as being the person responsible for the repainting of the original fourteenth-century ceiling and for the frieze on the upper part of the walls in the room situated in the northeast corner of the palace, next to the Sala Magna, which may perhaps be identified with the "cameram superiorem" in which the viceroy slept. In addition, in 1507 the painter Ferdinando de Rocca received payment "pro una pictora per eum facta in una tela pro camera illustris domini proregis in regio hospicii Panormi …" ("for a picture painted by him on a canvas for the room of the Illustrious Viceroy in the Royal Palace in Palermo"). In the same year the marbleworkers Antonio Vanello, Jacopo di Benedetto, and Giuliano Mancino are recorded as being employed at the palace, though it has not been possible to identify their works.

The great Scala Escuberta (Open Staircase), traces of

Right
A detail of the ceiling of the Sala Magna (Great Hall) on the second floor of the palace, painted between 1377 and 1380 by Simone da Corleone, Cecco di Naro, and Pellegrino De Arena da Palermo.

which still remain, dates from the second half of the fifteenth century or the early sixteenth century. A marble entrance overlooking the Piano della Marina, no longer in existence but visible in a seventeenth-century painting in the Museo Regionale in Palermo, may well date from the same period. When the tribunal of the Royal High Court was transferred to Palazzo Reale in 1598, Philip III granted Lo Steri to the Inquisition – previously based in the Castello a Mare – which had its seat there from 1601 to 1782, the year in which it was finally dissolved.

From 1783 the former residence of the Chiaramonte family housed the Refuge for the Poor of St. Dionysus, and, following that, the Royal Establishment for the Lottery. With the arrival of the Bourbon court at Palermo in 1798, the courts of the Consistory and the Royal High Court, previously based at Palazzo Reale, were moved to the upper floors of Lo Steri and the annexed Palazzo Abatellis, where they remained until 1958. During this period, the palace underwent further radical alteration, completed in 1800 by the architect Salvatore Attinelli. During the 1970s the palace was restored by the architect Roberto Calandra, with a view to making it the seat of the University Administration. On this occasion, the Venetian architect Carlo Scarpa was responsible for redesigning the entrance to correspond to the

eighteenth-century entrance on Piazza Marina attributed to the architect Giacomo Amato, as well as a number of external frames for the two-light Gothic windows and the doors onto the gallery on the first floor of the courtyard.

Castello Chiaramonte at Mussomeli

In the years that followed the Vespers uprising against the Angevins in 1282, Sicily was torn apart by civil wars. In the absence of the Aragonese kings, two factions struggled for power over the island – the *latina*, or "Latin" side, supported by Louis, the king of Naples, and led by the Palizzi and Chiaramonte families, and the *catalana*, or "Catalan" side, which backed the Aragonese kings and was led by, among others, the Alagona, Moncada, Ventimiglia and Peralta families.

Baronial conflicts and contests for power necessitated the construction of strongholds for territorial defense. The fourteenth century thus became the century par excellence for Sicilian feudal castles. Many grew out of pre-existing buildings, enlarged and altered, while others were newly built. The Chiaramonte family, which held sway over a large area of western Sicily, covered the Val di Mazzara, which they ruled almost exclusively, with fortified buildings. The most striking of these is the Castello di Mussomeli, which takes its name from the mountain which dominates the landscape.

In Book X of the first decade of *De rebus siculis decades*

Above and opposite
The imposing mass of the fortified castle of the Chiaramonte family, towering above the landscape of Mussomeli.

duae (Twenty Years of Sicilian History), which was published by Tommaso Fazello in 1558, in a paragraph entitled "The Valle di Mazara and its cities and castles," the historian states: "Eight miles away [from Cammarata] is castle Musumelli, erected by Manfredi di Chiaramonte, as recorded by the ancient letters above the door, from which it takes its name, 'Manfreda'. Though today it is called 'Montemele', from the mountain on which it is situated a mile away there is a fortress of the same name, built by the same man."

In the entry *Mussomeli* or *Mons mellis* in the *Dizionario topografico della Sicilia* (Topographical Dictionary of Sicily), published in 1856, Vito Amico adds one or two remarks to the information provided by Fazello. "At one time, the lord of the mountain was Corrado di Aurea. After this, it belonged to Manfredi di Chiaramonte, who built the village in a suitable place and erected the fortress on a cliff. The fortress, now in ruins, can be found a good mile away, still bearing the coat of arms of the Chiaramonte family."

The d'Auria, mentioned by Amico, has been identified as the Genoese Corrado I Doria, Admiral of Sicily, who from the beginning of the fourteenth century was lord of Castronovo, the region to which Mussomeli must have belonged. When Manfredi III Chiaramonte was granted the lordship of Castronovo by Frederick IV "The Simple",

he obtained dominion over Mussomeli, the name of which probably has Arab origins, like most Sicilian placenames.

The year 1374, the date of a letter written by Frederick IV "apud terram manfridae" (in the territory of Manfred), is the *terminus ante quem* for the

Opposite
The archway into the entrance hall beyond the second curtain of walls.

Below
Castello Chiaramonte.

founding of the village and the castle, where, between 11 and 20 November of that year, the king was Manfredi's guest. After staying in Palermo, waiting for the pope to agree to his coronation, the king made his way into the island's interior, with the intention of regaining dominion over the castles of his realm.

According to tradition, the Castello di Mussomeli hosted an assembly of barons in 1391, who gathered together from all over the island when it became clear that the Aragonese, who were intent on reclaiming Queen Maria's right to the throne, were about to invade Sicily. In the same year Manfredi died, leaving as his heir his son, Andrea, a man of little political aptitude. In 1392, the armed Aragonese landed on the island. A number of barons were accused of treachery, and Andrea himself was beheaded in front of his own Palermitan residence in Piazza Marina, his possessions having been appropriated by the Crown.

By a charter dated 4 April 1392, King Martin the Younger granted to Guglielmo Raimondo Moncada, Conte di Augusta, the countship of Malta, Gozo, and all the inhabited feuds that had formerly belonged to the Chiaramonte family, among them "castrum Musumelis cum terra Manfrele" ("Castello Mussomeli and the territory of Manfredi"). Five years later, in 1397, Moncada himself was declared a rebel. The lordship of Mussomeli

was then bestowed on Giacomo, Conte di Prades, the nephew of King James II of Aragon, who sold it by a deed of 1407 to Giovanni Castellar from Valencia, the royal treasurer. Around 1450 it passed to Giovanni di Perapertusa e Castellar, Barone di Favara, who, in 1451 was

obliged to sell the territory of Mussomeli to Federico Ventimiglia, Lord of Monforte, reserving the right to repurchase. Ventimiglia died two years later, leaving it to his son, Giovanni Giacomo, who was still a minor; it was therefore entrusted to Simone di Bologna.

During this period, Isabella Perapertusa, the daughter of Giovanni, had married the wealthy Pietro del Campo, who, in 1467, exercised his right to redeem the territory of Mussomeli. The last of this family to hold the lordship was Andreotto, who, being without children and heirs, sold it in 1549 to Don Cesare Lanza, Barone di Trabia e Castania. In 1563, he was the first to be granted the title of Conte di Mussomeli. The lordship remained in the possession of the Lanza family until the twentieth century.

The fortified complex of the Castello di Mussomeli is rendered unique by its extraordinary position at the top of an inaccessible cliff. It rises up from the surrounding countryside, with a sheer drop on all sides except the one by which it may be ascended – an ideal setting for legends and folk stories. Above all, the castle owes its singular fascination to its perfect blend of artifice and nature, where the rock on which it is built itself becomes an element of construction.

The castle is surrounded by a double curtain of walls. About thirty metres above the plain, an entrance with a pointed arch leads inside the first wall. Two eroded coats of arms are carved on the imposts of the arch, perhaps the arms of the Chiaramonte family. Proceeding up the slope one approaches the second curtain of walls, originally fourteenth-century, but later raised, and beyond them is the uncovered entrance hall. The arms of the Castellar family – three embattled towers – are carved above the doorway.

The castle is polygonal in form, its seven sides arranged in a pincer-like shape. The main body of the building looks onto the wall overhanging the southeast face, from which, according to folklore, convicted criminals were hurled to their deaths. The façade, composed of four sides, is continuous and embattled, and presents a series of two-light windows and two cylindrical towers positioned at the points where one side meets the other. Inside this main body there are a number of large rooms with an elegant finish, suggesting a residential rather than military function. It is reached by means of a Gothic doorway, which was completely restored during the twentieth-century, its arch decorated with the zigzag broken sticks pattern which, though already in use in the Palermo area in the Norman period and regarded variously as being of north-European or Islamic origin, became a leitmotiv of fourteenth-century Sicilian architecture.

The first room, the Sala dei Baroni (Hall of the

Barons), in which one presumes the assembly of 1391 took place, was probably covered at one time by a painted coffered wooden ceiling of the kind commissioned by Manfredi III for his Palermo palace in Piazza Marina between 1377 and 1380. Below this room is the Sala delle Armi (Hall of Weapons), which has a flat ceiling supported by five ogival arches.

A small triangular room, corresponding to the angle between the two sides of the polygon, was built to link the Sala dei Baroni with the next two rooms, the first of which is known as the Sala del Camino. These rooms are covered with cross-vaulting, supported by ribs standing on octagonal pillars, the capitals of which are decorated with a plant motif. A passageway leads to the last side of the building, consisting of a single room with a double cross-vault. This has a single pillar in three corners of the room, while the walls of the fourth corner and the floor are partly constituted by rock. The ribs of the two vaults stand on triple pillars, as does the arch separating the room into two bays. The design and the constructive modules of these rooms conform to models proper to Sicilian castle architecture in the time of Frederick, even with regard to certain decorative details, such as the rosette on the keystone at the crossing of the ribs of the vaults. New to Hohenstaufen architecture, however, are

certain constructive details typical of Sicilian churches and palaces of the late thirteenth and early fourteenth centuries, such as the octagonal section of the pillars in the rooms in the main body of the building.

According to the most recent studies by Giuseppe

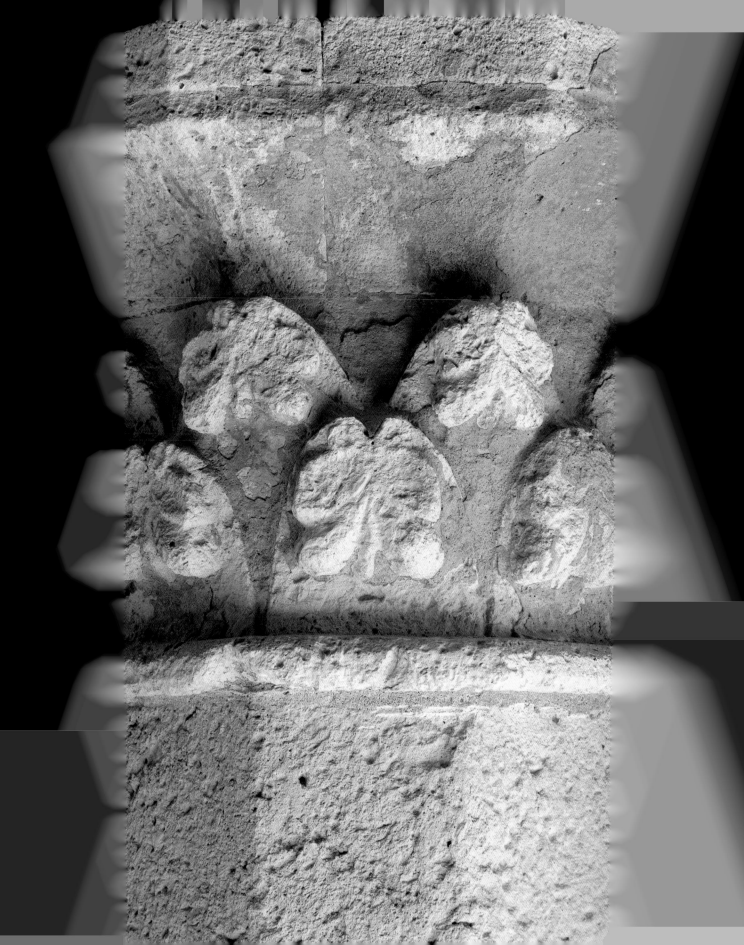

Spatrisano, the construction of the entire residential part of the building should be dated to the period of Corrado d'Auria, with the exception of the Sala dei Baroni, the only room which may be attributed to Manfredi III. The so-called Torre Mastra, the large, rectangular tower at the end of the wing on the right of the entrance and next to the castle wall, the summit of which is the highest point of the fortress, would appear to date from an even earlier period.

This part of the building also contains a chapel with a Gothic doorway, which was partially restored during the twentieth-century restoration works and is very similar to the doorway of the Sala dei Baroni. It is covered with a double cross-vault, the ribs of which rest, with the arch that separates the two bays, on triple pillars of rectangular section, a scheme already used in the Hohenstaufen Castello di Augusta. "Castrum est eminens, forte, pulchrum, cum par non invenitur in hac regione" ("The castle is conspicuous, strong, handsome, and has no equal in this region"), recorded Giovan Giacomo Adria, Charles V's doctor, in the first half of the sixteenth century. Abandoned at the end of that century, the Castello di Mussomeli was destined to remain almost intact – a unique example of fourteenth-century architecture that is at once imposing and refined.

Below
The arch of the high altar of the chapel rests on a capital carved with plant motifs.

Opposite
The ceiling of the chapel, with its double cross-vault.

Palazzo Termine-Pietratagliata in Palermo

For centuries, the Termine family was among the most important of all Catalan families who owned houses in Palermo. The Terminis originally came to Sicily with the first Kings of Aragon, or possibly even with the Swabian dynasty. According to local tradition, in 1209 Giovanni and Oliviero de Termens escorted Queen Constance of Aragon, the wife of Frederick II of Hohenstaufen, to the island. The Termine family held the highest civil, military and ecclesiastic posts on the island. In 1509 they became Baroni di Birribaida, in 1629 Principi di Casteltermine and, in 1769, they were made Principi di Baucina and Marchesi di Montemaggiore. The family died out during the second half of the nineteenth century when its titles and property passed through marriage to the Licata family.

The Termine family owned numerous houses scattered throughout the various districts of Palermo. One of these still stands today on Via Bandiera in the city's old quarter, close to the port. Since the thirteenth century, merchant communities had thrived in this area. Among the first to settle were the merchants from Malfi, then

Right
Giannizzo's drawing shows Palazzo Termine-Pietratagliata after the restoration work completed in the first half of the nineteenth century. It was then that balconies were added to the windows. The balconies were demolished at the beginning of the twentieth century.

Below right
The main elevation on Via Bandiera showing the corner window recreated at the start of the twentieth century on the evidence of what were presumed to be remains of a similar fifteenth-century arrangement.

Opposite
The tower dominates the elevation on Via Bandiera.

Genoa and Pisa. Following the Vespers, the Catalans came too. The whole area was therefore a flourishing hive of activity of every type. Later, the district became known as the Loggia. As the scholar Gaspare Palermo points out, this was because in the early nineteenth century around what is now Piazza del Garraffello, "there used to be two loggias, one where the Genoese and the other where the Catalans carried out their business".

Via Bandiera is one of the most ancient thoroughfares in Palermo's old city center. Until 1600, the year in which Strada Nova or Maqueda was opened, it ran uninterrupted through the city from Piazza del Capo to the sea. According to some sources, it got its name [which literally means Flag Street] from a "marble relief high on one corner that depicted a small putto or slave holding a standard". This corner was to be found where Via Bandiera meets the modern Via Patania. But Carmelo Piola advanced another theory in his *Dizionario sulle strade di Palermo* (Dictionary of Palermo Streets). According to Piola, the name derived from the flag that Matteo Termine used to hang from the windows of his house on the street. Matteo Termine was the Lord Chief Executioner and Captain General of Prisons under the Aragonese kings James and Frederick, that is to say during the latter part of the thirteenth century. There is, however,

Below
The Armory where the wooden ceiling was repainted with floral motifs during twentieth-century restoration work.

Opposite
A detail of the façade of Palazzo Oneto di Sperlinga seen from one of the windows of Palazzo Termine-Pietratagliata.

nothing to prove this theory. What is certain, though, is that Matteo meted out justice in a *palazzo* situated in the Albergheria quarter of town, where the Convent of Santa Chiara now stands. And it is now believed that the Termine house in Via Bandiera dates only from the fifteenth century.

The palazzo we see today was most probably the magnificent, private dwelling mentioned by the historian Pietro Ransano in his *Origini e vicende di Palermo* (Origins and stories of Palermo), written in around 1470. Ransano claims that the *palazzo* in question was built by the jurist "Antoni di Termini", in other words Antonio Termine e Ventimiglia. According to scholar Nino Basile, however, the building Ransano was referring to is more likely to have been the fifteenth-century palace that still stands near the Church of the Carmine. The façade of that building, in fact, still bears the carved crest of the Termine family. There used to be an inscription on the architrave over the entrance to the *palazzo* in Via Bandiera. Although it no longer exists, it was recorded by the seventeenth-century scholar Onofrio Manganante. The Latin inscription read. "Iesus Christi Operante Gratia, Antonius de Terminis Iurista Iudex Magnae Regiae Curiae Has Aedes Construxit Anno Salutis MCCCCCLXXII."

Basile dated the building from the late sixteenth century. He attributed its construction to Antonio Termine, a descendent of the

jurist of the same name cited by Ransano. This Antonio or, to give him his full name, Antonio Termine e Sabbia, Barone di Birribaida and High Court Judge of the Realm, lived in a time when Mannerism had pervaded Sicily. It is probable that he wanted to commission a

building reminiscent of the Chiaramonte style. The *palazzo* was therefore a deliberate revival which would thus remind everyone of the ancient origins of his family's power. If this is true, Basile's hypothesis also provides an explanation of the note Manganante made before he transcribed the epigraph. In the note Manganante commented that the *palazzo* "is

built in the old manner, as the materials and architecture show".

At the start of the nineteenth century the topographer and Arab scholar Salvadore Morso, writing in his *Descrizione di Palermo antico* (*Description of Ancient Palermo*), suggested that there was originally a Saracen or Norman building here. This has never been established. Today, however, it is difficult to refute the fifteenth-century foundation of the present building which was also put forward by Morso. This opinion was shared in his day by historian Gioacchino di Marzo.

Now that a proper stylistic assessment has been made, modern scholars believe they have narrowed the date in which construction started to sometime in the 1470s. They assume that the date of 1573, transcribed in some sources, was in fact 1473.

The *palazzo* mentioned by Ransano was therefore the residence on Via Bandiera. Although late nineteenth-century modifications now mask much of the earlier construction, the original features of this *palazzo* are undoubtedly Catalan Gothic, a style which swept Sicily between the end of the fifteenth and the start of the sixteenth centuries. The original structure was in square-cut stone with a tower to one side. Such a layout was totally in keeping with the tradition of residential building that was prevalent in Palermo during the fourteenth and

fifteenth centuries. Buildings tended to consist of a compact block. A cornice running right the way round the building between the floors rigidly subdivided the structure into two distinct orders. At some stage between the end of the nineteenth and the beginning of the twentieth century, the windows were radically altered. They do, however, still possess a few of their original features, in particular the archivolts mounted on carved corbels.

The building is still dominated by the "superb tower, the highest of all towers in Palermo" as a scholarly gentleman named Vincenzo Di Giovanni, writing an interesting manuscript entitled *Del Palermo Restaurato* (*Palermo Restored*), put it in 1615. At the end of the eighteenth century the Marchese di Villabianca also commented on the tower in his *Palermo d'Oggigiorno* (*Palermo Today*). He described it as "a tower of ancient build, with columns at the corners, which are signs of nobility and wealth."

Little evidence of the fifteenth century survives in the interiors. They were all completely refurbished midway through the eighteenth century. During this period, the Termine family became Principi di Baucina and Marchesi di Montemaggiore after the Migliaccio family died out. In 1748 they sold the house in Via Bandiera and moved to Palazzo Isnello dei Termine. The new owner of the Via Bandiera palace was Giovan Battista Marassi, a

member of a Venetian family that had settled in Sicily at the end of the seventeenth century, acquiring the barony of Fontanasalsa and the dukedom of Pietratagliata. It was Marassi who, in 1762, commissioned Vito D'Anna to paint a fresco showing *Il Trionfo del principe circondato dalle*

Virtù (The Triumph of the prince surrounded by the Virtues) on the ballroom ceiling. It was probably at the same time that the ballroom acquired its magnificent tiled floor, the 99-branch Murano chandelier and its *boiserie* in the French style. In later years, his best pupils, including his son Alessandro and brother-in-law Francesco Sozzi, assisted D'Anna who is also attributed with the celebratory fresco in what is now the dining room. The Red Room has a number of small views of Venice, which are probably references to the new owner's ancestry. The ceiling painting of *l'Allegoria della Saggezza* (the Allegory of Wisdom) was most likely carried out by Sozzi. He and D'Anna had already worked together at Palazzo Isnello in Palermo a few years earlier.

In 1818 Giovan Battista Marassi's only daughter married Don Luigi Alliata, the third son of the Principe di Villafranca. So it was that both the title of Duca di Pietratagliata and the *palazzo* in Via Bandiera passed to a new family. In 1828 the house had to be repaired and restored after earthquake damage five years earlier. The project was entrusted to the architect Nicolò Puglia. It is most likely during this period that work was carried out on the façade and balconies were added at the windows, as can be seen from drawings by M. Giarrizzo.

In the 1920s Francesco Valenti, who at the time held the post of Superintendent of Monuments, drew up plans for further restoration work. The famous Sicilian architect Ernesto Basile worked with him, but only with regard to the main fabric of the building. It was then that the windows along the main elevation were altered again. The balconies were removed while the windows themselves were given twin-light mullions. Catalan-style lunettes, with tracery-work and columns, provided the final touch. Basile and Valenti found what were presumed to be traces of jambs and arches. On this evidence they re-created *ex novo* a mullioned window on the corner. The entrance hall was refurbished in neo-Gothic style and the Armory was restored.

When the last of the Alliata di Pietratagliata family married the present Principe di Baucina a few years ago, Palazzo Termine returned to the possession of its ancient owners.

Right
Neo-Gothic style entrance dating from early twentieth-century restoration work.

Palazzo Ajutamicristo in Palermo

The Palazzo Ajutamicristo was built at the end of the fifteenth century within the context of the enthusiastic urban reappraisal that took place in various Sicilian cities, clearly the result of a period of great prosperity. Despite a succession of heavy restorations, the imposing palazzo is today still regarded as one of the most prestigious examples of late fifteenth-century Sicilian architecture. The street in which it stands is on the southern boundary of the Kalsa district of Palermo. The district covers approximately the area in which, between 937 and 938, the Arabs built a new citadel, distinct from the ancient Panormos, to defend themselves from popular unrest as well as enemy attack. The name Kalsa derives from al-Khalisa which means "the Elect". The district was reserved for the accommodation of the emir and his court, who occupied a more ancient seat of power, most probably the spot where the Norman kings built their seat of government.

The palazzo was built for Guglielmo Ajutamicristo, a member of one of the Pisa mercantile families who arrived in Sicily after 1406,

the year of the conquest of Pisa by Florence. The family had accumulated a considerable fortune through banking and trade, and this enabled them to acquire the barony of Calatafimi, until then in the possession of Donna Anna de Cabrera of the family of the Conti di Modica. Similarly, two years later the Ajutamicristos bought the fiefdom of Misilmeri, which formerly belonged to Giovanni Vincenzo La Grua. It was to consolidate his role as a member of the aristocracy that Guglielmo decided to have a sumptuous *domus magna* built in a part of the city that was then expanding, strategically situated for commerce. This was the old Via di Porta di Termini (now Via Garibaldi) which led those who entered the city into the Piazza della Fieravecchia (now Piazza Rivoluzione), site of an old market dating back to the thirteenth century or earlier.

The plans for the fifteenth-century palazzo comprised a three-storey building, of which the first floor was intended as storerooms for merchandise, the *piano nobile* as the living quarters of the owner, and the top floor as living quarters for the younger members of the family and the servants. The plans were entrusted to Matteo Carnilivari, an architect from Noto, who arrived in Palermo at the end of the 1480s, middle-aged and probably already well-known. In the same months, the powerful Abatellis family

also turned to Carnilivari for the construction of their palazzo in the Via Alloro. Trained in Noto, Carnilivari brought to Palermo a culture rich in features of the late Spanish Gothic. In the fifteenth century, and thus before the destruction caused by the earthquake of 1693, Noto must have been similar architecturally to nearby Syracuse, the seat since 1361 of the Camera Regionale, dowry of the queens of Aragon and hence a place to which aristocratic Catalan families swarmed, and to which Catalan artists were summoned to satisfy their demands.

If the severe, massive grandeur of the residence of Guglielmo Ajutamicristo belongs to the Sicilian tradition of palace architecture, many other elements, some of which survive, attest to the enormous influence, more or less direct, of Catalan Gothic culture in Sicily.

Elements of this artistic fusion are easily identifiable on the façade. Several windows that are clearly original survive on the top storey, characterized by depressed longitudinal arches surmounted by substantial hoodmoulds with pendent capitals, while only a few traces of the Catalan Gothic windows with one opening remain between the grandiose architraved balconies of the *piano nobile* added between the end of the sixteenth century and the early years of the seventeenth. Apart from the clear Iberian references of the

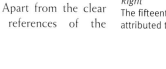

Right
The fifteenth-century arcade is attributed to Matteo Carnilivari.

hood-mould shaped like a basket arch, the windows of the first mezzanine, largely rebuilt and elongated downwards, confer just a touch of novelty. The first signs of the Italian Renaissance are seen in the marble parts of the jambs and lintels, where pairs of putti support the coat of arms of the Ajutamicristo family. Although the Renaissance was already flourishing in the north of Italy, it began to spread to Sicily thanks to the presence of several outstanding sculptors, including Domenico Gagini and Francesco Laurana, both of whom arrived during the 1460s after long experience in contact with the Italian peninsula. The colonnade, with a double arcade on one side of the internal courtyard, is also the result of the same complex artistic ambience, born of the fusion of local and Iberian culture with the recent experiments in northern Italy. It was probably furnished originally with an open stairway that led to the *piano nobile*, as was usual in Catalan houses and in Catalan-style dwellings built in Sicily, including the Palazzo Bellomo in Syracuse and the Palazzo Abatellis in Palermo. The arcade consists of five polycentric arches with cautious attempts at creating Renaissance capitals on the lower level and seven bays with ogive arches on the upper level of the internal walls which display perfectly preserved windows with two lights in the Catalan Gothic style. Together with the main entrance – crowned with the

Ajutamicristo coat of arms – the arcade is the most complete part left of the work of Carnilivari at the palazzo, assisted by craftsmen of diverse backgrounds and training. Of these, Giovanni Casada from Majorca, the Sicilian Nicolò Galizia, Bernardo Bevilacqua from Palermo, and

the Sardinian Antioco di Cara worked on the external stone carving, on the doorways, windows and arches; the marble workers Giacomo de Benedetto and Andrea de Curso made the stairs; and craftsmen from Noto, Messina, Ferrara (Alessandro Rubino), and France (Giovanni Burgognon) also worked at the palazzo. The presence of Gabriele di Battista from Como, a bearer of the artistic idiom of the Renaissance to Sicily, is also documented: he worked on the modelled decorations of the palazzo, probably with Andrea Mancino.

The interiors of the palazzo have been profoundly altered by the addition of false ceilings and partitions that obscure remarkable painted wooden ceilings, and have now lost all their fourteenth-century characteristics. From 1588, the year in which Francesco Moncada, Principe di Paternò and Duca di Montalto acquired the palazzo, it underwent several phases of intervention which involved the modification of the existing fabric of the building and the addition of new parts including the present grand staircase. With aristocratic extravagance the same Francesco Moncada saw to the augmentation of the *domus magna* "nella mole, negli ornamenti" ("of the massive building itself and of the decorative elements"). According to the description of the palazzo compiled by Gaspare Palermo, author of the *Guida istruttiva per Palermo e i suoi*

dintorni, published in 1816, "there are splendid apartments in the upper storeys, reception rooms, galleries with pictures, gilding, stucco and other types of ornamentation, with splendid adornments, and costly foreign wall hangings in the most refined taste …" This statement probably refers to the renovations ordered in the second half of the seventeenth century by Don Aloisio Moncada, Principe di Paternò, grandee of Spain and peer of the realm, for the modernization of the "grand part" of the palazzo.

The reconstruction work included the modernization of the "minor part" including the private apartments of the prince, where, between 1764 and 1768, the architects Nicolò Anito and Andrea Gigante worked, together with a team of plasterers and stucco workers, painters, marble workers and stonecutters. Gigante undertook the construction *ex novo* of a part of the building furnished with a new entrance, and in which the ballroom opening on to the terrace was built between 1763 and 1766. From 1773, documents indicate the presence of Giuseppe Venenzio Marvuglia, the architect who was mainly responsible in Sicily for the diffusion of the Neoclassic, which he had absorbed in the course of a long stay in Rome. The fashion for the Neoclassic was in opposition to the taste for the Rococo, whose origins were French and which, in the 1770s, was still favoured

in the decoration of several Palermo salons. Marvuglia worked on a T-shaped part of the building – at right angles to the fifteenth-century part – which included new quarters for the princess. From 1880 to 1881 a few artists collaborating with the architect were employed in the decoration of several reception rooms: the Neapolitan perspective painter Benedetto Cotardi painted "the perspective wall painting in the dining room and that in the drawing room of the new apartment". These paintings can most likely be identified with the illusionist architectural painting of the dining room and with that in the stucco-framed panels in the aforesaid ballroom, also known as the *camerone*. The painter Giuseppe Crestadoro, pupil of Vito D'Anna and listed as working on the rebuilding of the palazzo as early as the 1760s, was charged with executing the figurative paintings in many of the rooms.

Of those cited in documents, "the figures on the walls and ceilings of the dining room" may be identified with the nudes placed within the painted illusionist architecture of that room while "[the figures] in the six oil paintings for the ornamental panels over the doors" refer to those of the *camerone* or ballroom, on the ceiling of which the same artist signed the "Gloria del principe virtuoso".

Gaspare Palermo also records that the portraits of the family painted by Pietro Novelli were hung in the dining room, and that the palazzo was at one time surrounded by a large garden "largely embellished and dignified with covered, tree-lined walks, fountains, statues and seats, which, due to the generosity of Don Giovan Luigi Moncada, was open to the public, who could stroll there in summer as well as in winter." The list of illustrious personages who stayed or visited there highlights the splendor of this magnificent palazzo, now owned by the Calefati family, baroni di Canalotti. The Marchese di Villabianca wrote: "The palazzo Ajutamicristo is ultimately renowned for the *apossento* [the apartments that were reserved for royalty and the royal household when in residence] where Giovanna, queen of Naples stayed in 1500, the Emperor Charles V in 1535, and Muleassen, king of Tunisia in 1544." From 1567 to 1620, the Accademia dei Cavalieri and the Accademia degli Accesi, patronized by the viceroy, the Marchese di Pescara, had their seat in a wing of the palazzo.

Preceding pages
Detail of the fresco in the dining room: the figures are painted by Giuseppe Crestadoro and the architectural perspectives by Benedetto Cotardi. The corbels visible at the top of the photograph were recently uncovered and belong to the original ceiling, which survives but is obscured by the frescoed eighteenth-century ceiling.

Right
Detail of the ceiling of one of the salons, decorated with landscape paintings set in gilt stucco frames.

Villa San Marco in Santa Flavia

In Sicily, the origins of the custom of taking holidays in the country can be traced, according to recent research, to the Saracen and the Norman periods. There is good reason to think that structures such as the Castello di Maredolce, la Zisa or la Cuba may be shown to be the precursors of the later extra-mural architecture that sprang up in the environs of Palermo in the seventeenth and eighteenth centuries. It is thus possible to reconstruct the outlines of the evolution of the villa on the island. Continuing without interruption from the medieval period, it followed its own course, the foreign influences combining with those of local architectural models, fortified or rural, as well as sometimes – from the sixteenth century onwards – local villas sharing features with examples from the Italian peninsula. From these two sources – the local one and that imported from the mainland – a type of suburban architecture emerged that is typically Sicilian and which came to be eminently suited to the social and political life of the island aristocracy. Maps from the beginning of the eighteenth century show many villas and country

Above
The main façade of the villa San Marco.

Opposite
The double external staircase commissioned in 1673 to be designed by the Dominican friar Andrea Cirrincione. On the right, one of the portals of the curtain wall.

houses near Palermo and Messina, in the surroundings of Catania and in the coastal area to the north of that city, and also in the surroundings of Syracuse and of other centres of the Val di Noto.

The Marchese di Villabianca wrote that Bagheria had primacy over the whole Palermo countryside, for the open air to be enjoyed there and for the extent of its surroundings. It also takes supremacy for the splendour of its palazzi and villas, which adorn the area magnificently. There are various opinions as to the etymology of the name. The marchese thought it originated from the Arabic *Bagarìa*, "meaning sandy soil," while "one might say Baccarìa, in honor of Bacchus, because of the wonderful wines that they have there." According to the historian Gioacchino Di Marzo, it is more likely that Bagheria means "maritime region", since the Arabic word *bahr* means "sea – and the spit of land that juts out between the bay of Palermo and that of Termini is to a great extent enclosed by the sea."

The presence of medieval castles is documented in the region of Bagheria, as – from as early as the middle of the fourteenth century – is the presence of the *masseria*, a type of fortified rural building whose purpose was originally agricultural, but in which a part of the building was retained as the country home of the owner. At this time, and until the seventeenth century, the distinction between the *masseria* and the villa was not yet very clear-cut; even later on, the villa in many cases kept some characteristics of the *masseria*, the main one being the *baglio*, a group of low buildings set around a closed courtyard, an arrangement that originated in the Saracen period. The Villa Valdina, located between Solanto and Bagheria, is an example; its surviving frescoes, painted in the 1620s by Pietro Novelli, attest to the residential use of the villa at that time.

According to the account written by the Marchese di Villabianca, family tradition has it that, in the 1650s, Giuseppe Branciforte, Principe di Pietraperzia and Conte di Raccuia, began to build the villa of Bagheria where he then long resided, content to be far from the city. He did not want to appear at court, where he found the Spanish viceroys too grand and therefore distanced himself from their entourage. As a result, his villa later attained supremacy – previously held by the large house – over all the villas which had recently sprung up in Bagheria. It was known with good reason as the *casena grande* and the oldest in Bagheria. It could be described as a baronial palazzo, since it ruled a populous domain called Raccuia nuova, commonly known as Butera.

The original, deliberately archaic, fortified façade of the Villa Branciforte – later known as Butera – was transformed by the reconstruction in the second half of the

eighteenth century. The original façade served as a defense against possible popular revolt, but the main reason for its appearance was one of taste. In Sicily, as in the rest of Italy, the military appearance of country houses was attained by using certain elements such as rustication, bastions, towers and crenellations; these were adopted during the Renaissance from aesthetic preference, but this was not without certain socio-political implications. By means of its antique appearance, the villa-castello became a symbol of the old nobility and of power. Sicily, especially, gloried in a long tradition of such buildings, and the austere and geometrically compact forms of its extramural Norman dwellings were handed on down the centuries.

The construction of the Branciforte villa played a fundamental part in the later development of Bagheria as a place of *villeggiatura*, or escape to the country, of the aristocracy. Beginning in the 1660s, new dwellings sprang up extremely quickly, sometimes utilizing existing shells of houses or towers. Extant structures were used in building the villas of the Sollimas, Marchesi di Santa Marina, the Lo Fasos, Duchi di Serradifalco, and the Filangeris, Conti di San Marco. The land of the Conti di San Marco was in Val Demone. According to historiography, Roberto il Guiscardo, the Norman, built a castle there in 1061 on the site of ancient Alunzio. Under Frederick II of Hohenstaufen it belonged to the Rossos, from whom it later passed to Riccardo Filangeri through marriage. Later still it belonged to Sancio of Aragon, illegitimate son of Frederick of Aragon, whose descendent Frederick

Preceding pages
The upper part of the staircase that leads, via a drawbridge, to the main entrance.

Below and opposite
The well and the stone table and benches within the walled courtyard.

was accused of felony by King Martin. King Martin confiscated Frederick's assets and awarded the feudal state and the castello di San Marco to Abbo Filangeri, alcalde of Cefalù and Maestro Razionale (chief communal administrator) of the kingdom. Abbo Filangeri's great-grandson Riccardo was the first to be awarded the title of Conte di San Marco by charter, by King Alfonso in 1453.

In the times of the Marchese di Villabianca, the Filangeris of San Marco owned a magnificent villa at Bagheria, the second oldest of the villas in the region. At its centre it had a fortified tower, with drawbridges, in the manner of a fortress in order to resist the incursions of the Turks at that time. The fortified appearance of this villa-castello, with its massive cubic construction reinforced with corner bastions, is still in evidence. The presence of the tower at the centre compensated for the fact that it was not situated on high ground and enabled it to control the surrounding territory just the same. Similar architectural models had appeared during the sixteenth century in central Italy and such villas could have spread to Sicily by means of architectural treatises.

The Villa San Marco, initiated by Vincenzo Giuseppe Filangeri, the first Principe di Mirto, was almost certainly built according to plans by the Dominican friar Andrea Cirrincione. He was active in the seventeenth

century in Palermo, where he worked on the sites of the churches of S. Domenico and S. Cita. He was also responsible for the first plan of the villa of the Principe di Resuttano in the district of Colli. In several documents dated 1673, this architect also appears to be responsible for

the "great staircase which was to be built in the new Casino [villa] of the illustrious Signore, the Conte di San Marco." From this, it may be

Opposite
The room with the cistern, with the old kitchens annexed, on the ground floor of the villa.

Below
The main entrance hall or sala d'armi on the piano nobile.

deduced that the villa had only recently been built, bearing in mind that a few earlier defensive works were incorporated. The double flight of stairs, which rises in a broken curvilinear design only to be reunited in a single straight section, was probably finished in 1678. Built at a

On the ground floor, beneath the entrance hall, is the room containing the cistern; the old kitchens are laid out around this room. At the time the villa was built, it was surrounded by a court-yard enclosed by a wall; built against this wall on two sides were the service buildings,

Left
Decorative details of the walls and ceiling of the dining room.

certain distance from the main entrance to the *piano nobile* on the second level, the stairs are connected to this entrance via a drawbridge, another sign of homage to the taste for fortified structures. In the large entrance hall, several pieces from the rich collection of weapons cited in an inventory of the posses-sions of the family dating back to 1724, are still preserved. Around the entrance hall are the recep-tion rooms; their arrangement dates back to an eighteenth-century restoration.

and at the back a large chapel. The curtain wall is broken at the centre of each of its four sides by a stone portal – three arched and the fourth polygonal – sur-mounted by pinnacles, deco-rations and geometric motifs stylistically similar to those of the staircase.

Villa De Simone-Wirz in Palermo

When he was describing the countryside around Palermo, the Marchese di Villabianca paid particular attention to the Colli plain. "The broad and pleasant Palermitan meadowland is known as Colli because it rises gently in the manner of a hill. It lies at the feet of four mountains, Pellegrino, Gallo, Belampo, and Billiemi, and is twelve miles long, including the six miles of the lower slopes of mounts Pellegrino and Billiemi. Colli has a pleasant air and is second only to Bagheria among the grander parts of the countryside around Palermo. This is due to the magnificent mansions and villas that enhance the area. It is also where Palla and Pomona have their favorite abode."

From the middle of the seventeenth century onwards and, in particular, during the following century, a phenomenal number of residential buildings sprang up across the Colli, as had occurred at both Mezzo Monreale and Bagheria. The aristocratic Sicilian families who, at the end of the previous century had moved back to the capital to pay court to the viceroy, competed in the level of luxury and refinement and, to

Right
The armorial bearings of the La Grua Talamanca family.

Below
One façade of the rectangular courtyard called a *baglio*. The staircase leads to the *piano nobile*.

Opposite
The eighteenth-century archway that leads into the *baglio*.

prove the eminence of their family names, built imposing palazzi in the town and sumptuous villas in the country. At Bagheria, the country houses of the upper echelons of the aristocracy, culminating in the Brancifortes, sprang up *ex novo*. But the Colli plain also accommodated the country houses of members of the professional middle classes. Here the building frenzy was focused – with the exception of a few sporadic instances, in particular, by the villa of the Principe di Resuttano – on the transformation of shells of rustic buildings with exclusively agricultural origins, sometimes fortified to face the danger of incursions of sea pirates. Sometimes Norman garden buildings were incorporated in new villas, as occurred at Villa Cuba

Above
The entrance hall of the *piano nobile* with the blue-and-white tiled floor.

Right
The coffered wooden ceiling of the entrance hall, decorated with vegetal and floral motifs. The putti painted on the frieze support a hanging with the arms of the La Grua Talamanca family.

Soprana. In fact, part of Colli was developed on the very plain that the Altavillas had gradually transformed into their own royal park. It consisted of gardens of delight, like a small Islamic paradise on earth.

An extraordinary example of the transformation of a rustic structure into a grand residence is the Villa De Simone-Wirz, whose first nucleus – to which the two large towers that lean against the central building might well have belonged – was the property of Francesco Castrone in the seventeenth century, according to several recent studies. The villa afterwards belonged to Giulio Maria Pollastra and then to the La Grua Talamancas, Principi di Carini.

The original core of the building dates back to 1534, and constitutes the oldest building in the region of Partanna, a mountain spur at the extreme limit of the northeastern boundary of the Colli. This area belonged to the La Grua Talamanca family in the seventeenth century; at the beginning of the eighteenth century it passed through marriage to the Graffeo family, Principi di Partanna, who built the nearby Villa Partanna, one of the finest examples of the Rococo in the Colli plain.

A drive with numerous exotic plants and citrus trees leads into the English park that surrounds the villa. One passes under an archway to the courtyard at the centre of the building. Although the

Below and opposite
The dining room on the *piano nobile* with its painted wooden ceiling, frescoed walls and tiled floor.

fruit of continuous adaptations and modifications that have complicated the plan by the addition of secondary courtyards, the architectural whole is founded on a basic design often used in country houses in the surroundings of Palermo: a main building with the grandest elevations and, at right angles to the ends of this, two wings consisting of a series of low buildings used as storerooms and stables. These service buildings form a rectangular courtyard, which, in Sicilian country houses, is called a *baglio*. This basic scheme which was, in its original form, simple and exclusively agricultural in purpose, dates back to the Saracen period, but later underwent a slow transformation over the centuries, until it became a leitmotif of country architecture, an essential and unfailing part of a good many stately eighteenth-century villas.

The outside of the Villa De Simone-Wirz has a sober and rather elegant sixteenth-century appearance, rendered more graceful in the following century by the addition of two archways leading into the courtyard and of the grand double stairway with pierced balustrades which leads, in a curvilinear movement, to the *piano nobile*. The impressive entrance hall is surrounded by the other rooms of the *piano nobile*. In a few of these, the seventeenth- to eighteenth-century decorations are perfectly preserved: rustic coffered ceilings with decorative motifs painted in tempera and which date from the seventeenth

century, painted friezes on the upper parts of the walls in the sixteenth-century Roman manner representing the arms of the La Grua Talamancas interspersed with panels containing landscapes supported by putti, and floors paved with small blue-and-white ceramic tiles that formed a zig-zag

Opposite
An ornamental panel over a doorway, painted in fresco on a wall of the dining room; it depicts a medallion with a vase of flowers that rests on a *trompe l'œil* corbel with volutes.

Below
A corner of the dining room, leading into the entrance hall.

pattern – all forms of decoration prevalent in the eighteenth century.

The first floor contains a series of rooms with rib vaults; these were modified in the eighteenth century, judging by the coat of arms of the La Grua Talamanca family painted on the keystone of the vault of the central room. The stucco decoration with Rococo motifs of the chapel of the Holy Crucifix dates from the middle of the eighteenth century; access to the chapel is through the small portico on its external façade, added in the twentieth century to provide the terrace above it.

Following the La Grua Talamancas, in the middle of the nineteenth century, the villa came became the property of monsignor Nicolò Bignardelli, a relative of the princes of Partanna; he left it to his niece Achates Blanco, wife of the Barone De Simone. The villa eventually came into the hands of its present owners with the marriage of Maria Stella De Simone to the Conte Wirz.

Above and right
The eighteenth-century chapel decorated with frescoes and gilded stucco.

Palazzo Butera in Palermo

During the second half of the sixteenth century, a series of important urban renewal schemes gave rise to the radical transformation of Palermo from a medieval and Saracen city into a modern, monumental one. As well as encouraging the straightening and lengthening of the main street, the present Corso Vittorio Emmanuele, previously known as Strada Marmorea or Strada Cassaro, Marcantonio Colonna undertook the paving of the *strada del mare*, which was named Strada Colonna after him. This street ran on top of the curtain wall, the defensive wall of the city; access to the city from the Strada Colonna was at that time via two gates: the Porta dei Greci which is still standing, and the Porta del Molo, later rebuilt.

In 1593, on the occasion of the entry of the relics of S. Ninfa, one of the four patrons of the old city, a length of defensive wall was torn down, and there, a few decades later, the Porta Felice was built in honour of Donna Felice Orsini, the wife of Marcantonio Colonna.

The so-called *passeggiata a mare* (promenade on the sea front) became a meeting place for members of Palermo

Above
Royal Cavalcade for the entry of Charles III into Palermo. Detail of an engraving by Giuseppe Vasi (1736). The Palazzo Butera can be identified among the palazzi overlooking the promenade on the sea front.

Opposite
The façade of the Palazzo Butera that faces the sea appears above a long terrace located at the level of the *piano nobile*.

society, and there too, spectacles and concerts took place, as recorded in seventeenth-century sources. In 1681, a loggia for "musical entertainments" – designed by Paolo Amato, one of the greatest architects of the time – was built just by the Porta Felice. The loggia was known as the

Strada Colonna, along the top of the wall, was called Strada delle Cattive. According to tradition, it was reserved for the *captivae*, the Latin word for "widows" who, unwilling to renounce the pleasures and the worldly obligations of the sea shore, met one another undisturbed in this secluded spot.

"marble theatre by the shore" and, as revealed by old engravings, it was flanked by two fountains, while many statues and *trompe l'œil* frescoes with arches and columns decorated the city wall. The promenade that today runs parallel to

It was quite a panorama that could once have been enjoyed from the terraces of the Palazzo Butera, one of the most majestic palazzi of Palermo. Imposing in its proportions, it extended along a good part of the

promenade on the front, above the city walls. The present structure was formed by the union of several buildings incorporated into its central core between the eighteenth century and the beginning of the nineteenth.

In 1692, the Duchi di Branciforte, Marchesi di Martini and cadet branch of the family of the Principi di Scordia, representatives of the oldest and most powerful part of the Sicilian aristocracy, acquired a group of houses and transformed them into a palazzo which they proceded to use as their main residence. In 1718 the duke Ercole Michele married Caterina Branciforte-Ventimiglia, who, as her father's only heir, was invested with the title of Principessa di Butera. The two branches of the family were united, and the palazzo acquired its present name.

In the first half of the eighteenth century, the palazzo was rebuilt, apparently according to a plan by Giacomo Amato. A few designs relating to the transformation of the"casino of his excellency the Duca di Branciforti" by this architect must predate his death in 1732. The first two refer to the plan of the palazzo before and after the changes proposed by Amato; if these are compared with the present arrangements, it would seem that they were carried out more or less in their entirety. The third, relating to the "modern façade of the casino in the strada di S. Nicolò la Calsa

[the present Via Butera] of the most excellent Signor, the Duca di Branciforti", on the other hand, shows a different distribution of doors and windows; furthermore, these are typologically different from the present, clearly eighteenth-century doors and windows on this façade. An

Below
Detail of a fresco on the ceiling of the Salone di Apollo, portraying a young lady.

Opposite
A corner of one of the drawing rooms of the piano nobile, showing the architectural perspectives on the frescoed ceiling. The floor is paved with polychrome tiles.

engraving in La Reggia in trionfo per l'acclamazione della Sacra Reale Maestà di Carlo Infante di Spagna (The Palace in Triumph for the Acclamation of His Royal Highness Charles, Infante of Spain) published in 1735 shows the façade facing the sea, decorated for a holiday, proving that, at that time, the elevations had assumed their present form stylistically, and that the other

external alterations were directed almost exclusively at adding on buildings. In 1760, the palazzo of the Conte di Caltanissetta was annexed, and in 1801 that of Francesco Benso. The latter looked out on the Porta Felice; its façades were gradually altered to conform to the main building and its rooms were suitably decorated.

As for the interiors, documents record several names in connection with decorations carried out during various phases of rebuilding. Between 1728 and 1730, during the period when the architect Ferdinando Fuga was in charge of the rebuilding, and from 1734 to 1736, under the direction of the engineer Giuseppe Li Gotti – who has also been suggested as the author of the present façades – many plasterers and stucco workers (Domenico Guastella), carvers (Giovanni Battista Rizzo), and painters (Pietro Martorana, Rosario Berna and Olivio Sozzi) worked on the enterprise.

Scholars, however, assume that no trace of these decorations remained after the ruinous fire of 1759, which was followed by fifty years of restoration and redecoration. For these later restorations – directed first by the architect Paolo Vivaldi (1765–7), then by the engineer Salvatore Attinelli (1779–81), and finally by the engineer Carlo Chenchi and the architect Pietro Trombetta (after 1799) – the documents often cite little-known names, and it is now difficult to identify the work done by these men. There were a good number of plasterers and stucco workers (Francesco Alajmo and Domenico Guastella) and specialized painters. Many of these were painters of ornamental motifs and perspective painters (Gaspare and Giuseppe Cavaretta and Benedetto Cotardi); the figurative painters cited include Giuseppe Burgio and Gaspare Vizzini – the latter painted ornamental panels over doorways with ordinary peasant subjects as well as portraits – and, above all, the better known Emanuele and Elia Interguglielmi, who received payment between 1800 and 1806. At least some of the splendid frescoes in the reception rooms of the Palazzo Butera should be attributed to these two – the frescoes are perhaps the most perfect examples of the figurative painting of the second half of the eighteenth century and the very beginning of the nineteenth century in Sicily. Traditionally, however, these were attributed by authoritative eighteenth- to nineteenth-century sources to Gioacchino Martorana and now dated to the 1780s.

An elegant red marble staircase with graceful columns that support the cross vault leads into the palace. The entrance hall on the *piano nobile* has a frescoed ceiling painted with angels and putti that support the coat of arms of the Brancifortes. Many portraits of members of the family hang on the walls, while views of the many

Right
Detail of the frescoed ceiling of the Salone di Apollo, portraying a young nobleman.

domains and estates of the powerful family of the Principi di Butera are painted in the ornamental panels over the doors. The ceilings of the reception rooms, which lead into one another, were decorated according to the fashion of the period with a prevalence of *trompe l'œil*, aimed at the creation of grandiose effects whose purpose was to disconcert the spectator. In these demonstrations of perspective technique, the elegant figures that lean over the false balustrades are drawn from a rich repertory of arcadian and exotic motifs: they include the Turk and the little Japanese lady, young knights and ladies accompanied by devoted pages, fishermen and fisherwomen with nets, young lads and children absorbed in playful activities, such as blowing soap bubbles. Portrayed with the aid of a particularly fine range of colors, these images could in theory be said to approach the fashion which, side by side with official culture, was popular around Naples, giving rise to the decorations of the private villas near Vesuvius, Portici and Herculaneum.

Representations of subjects from classical mythology – *Diana the Huntress on her Chariot* symbolizing the moon, and *Apollo with the Chariot of the Sun* respectively – triumph at the centre of the ceiling of the Gothic *salone* and of that in the adjacent *salone*. The ceiling of the last *salone* was decorated, however, in stucco with typical curvilinear cornices consisting of vegetal

Below
Frescoed ceiling of the Salone di Apollo with Apollo on the Chariot of the Sun at its centre, surrounded by *trompe l'œil* architectural painting.

Opposite
Shepherd with Dog, detail of a fresco on the ceiling of a reception room on the *piano nobile*.

motifs interspersed with putti. A few rooms on the next floor have frescoed ceilings of considerable quality, with allegorical figures symbolizing the planets: Mercury and Venus, Jupiter and Mars, the Sun and Saturn.

The succession of *saloni* that run along behind the façade that faces the sea looks out on a wide terrace which, uniquely, runs without interruption above the Strada delle Cattive. The charm of this place and of the panorama that could be enjoyed from it did not fail to exert its influence on Goethe, who stayed in an apartment in the palazzo during his sojourn in Palermo. On the second of April 1787 he noted in his diary that "We rejoiced in the infinitely varied landscape and tried to fix it in our memories, drawing and sketching in detail; here, an artist could gather an inexhaustible harvest." And again: "The clear moonlight captivated us, in the evening … and, after we had returned, we stayed on the balcony for a long time. The play of light was singular in the extreme, and great the stillness and the enchantment."

Villa Valguarnera at Bagheria

The eighteenth century was the golden age of building at Bagheria, which had been favored by the aristocracy for the construction of their country houses since the previous century. Early in the eighteenth century, work started on the building of two significant villas, namely Villa Valguarnera and Villa Palagonia, the most notable and original examples of the architecture of Bagheria. According to sources, the Villa Valguarnera was founded by Maria Anna Gravina, daughter of the Principe di Gravina, first married to Giuseppe Valguarnera, Conte di Assoro and Principe di Valguarnera and Gangi, and married for the second time to Giuseppe Del Bosco, Principe di Cattolica. The present villa is, however, the result of a series of rebuilding schemes that continued throughout the eighteenth century. The Marchese di Villabianca writes: "Her sons and heirs, one by one, all fired by a munificent sense of competition, constantly ennobled it by bestowing on it the beauty and distinction of its present superb form." It thus became "the pinnacle of all the villas and delightful abodes of the great lords of Palermo."

Above
Villa Valguarnera in a fresco painted on the wall of a room in the Palazzo Valguarnera-Gangi in Palermo.

Opposite
An archway leading into the *baglio* that surrounds the villa.

The Marchese added: "Its elevated position ... placed it at the summit of grandeur to which a villa might aspire." Maria Anna had in fact acquired a small *montagnola*, a hill two or three hundred metres high on which to build her country house; this gave it a dominant position in relation to the other aristocratic residences in the area, particularly to those of the Brancifortes, Principi di Butera, with whom her family had strong links. The villas were opposite each other; moreover, the marriage between Maria Anna's first-born, Francesco Saverio Valguarnera, and Agata Branciforte, daughter of the Principe di Butera, sealed the alliance between the two powerful families.

Unlike the seventeenth-century villas built in the area, the Villa Valguarnera was conceived as independent of any agricultural function: it was simply an annex in the country to the palazzo in town, a seat of pomp and frivolity in relative seclusion, a manifestation of the power and decorum of the family, all in accordance with the outlook of the new century. There are two contracts dated September 1712: one for the construction and one for the carving of the stone for the outside of the villa. The first names the Dominican architect Tommaso Maria Napoli as author of the plans and the model; the second was entrusted to the master Antonino Perricone. Padre Napoli was also responsible

for the selection of the hill on which to build the new villa. He had lived and worked in Rome, at the Bourbon court, in Vienna, Dubrovnik, and, as a military architect, in Hungary for prince Eugene of Savoy. It is to him that the conception of a building, which recalls Roman Baroque

models and examples from the great courts of Europe, should undoubtedly be attributed.

If the *baglio* that surrounds the main entrance courtyard is typically Sicilian, its shape has close affinities with particular mainland Italian models. The wings, which, on leaving the villa embrace the courtyard in an oval, call to mind the Bernini colonnade of St Peter's in Rome. The end of the seventeenth century and the beginning of the eighteenth was a time of great resonance for the work

Above
The coat of arms of the Valguarnera family at the top of the main façade.

Opposite
The main façade of the villa, seen from the hill, with the grand staircase and the *baglio* that consists of low service buildings with flat roofs that serve as terraces.

of Bernini. Carlo Fontana, an architect to whom Padre Napoli must have been closely linked, repeated the plan of the colonnade in the plans for the reconstruction of the Palazzo Montecitorio in Rome. Padre Napoli was the first to use Bernini's example in a country villa, but it is worth remembering that there were already a few Palladian buildings whose courtyards were embraced by two wings.

Although the construction of the Villa Valguarnera continued even after the death of its first architect in 1725, and the deaths of Maria Anna and Giuseppe Del Bosco who comissioned it, it is probable that these further stages of work were, however, directed at completing the original plans. However, documents relate that, five years later, when Francesco Saverio Valguarnera, Principe di Valguarnera and first son of Maria Anna, entrusted the marble workers Gaspare Ferro and Francesco Lanza to finish the two wings of the main courtyard and the *parterre* in front of the main entrance, the façade facing the sea and the garden had already been completed. The inventory compiled following the death of Francesco Saverio in 1739 shows that even the interiors were already elegantly furnished.

From 1739 to 1740, the architect Emanuele Caruso of the Order of the Fathers of St. Camillus was charged with assessing the work already done on the building

and restoration of the balustrades of the villa, and to bring it to completion not only in the *parterre*, but also along the staircase and in the courtyard.

New and significant restorations succeeded one after the other from the middle of the eighteenth century onwards. A first *tranche* of work was commissioned by Pietro Valguarnera, who busied himself with the building of the new wing of the Palazzo Valguarnera-Gangi in Palermo at the same time. From 1748 to 1750, the villa was restored under the direction of the young architect Giovanni Del Frago, who may have been trained in Naples. He put the finishing touches to all four façades, with pilasters, architraves, friezes, cornices in imitation marble, panels in turquoise and with the "shield and the coat of arms of their lordships with colored banners and trophies ..." A similar design, in simplified form, was carried out on the external walls of the courtyard and under the balustrades, while other parts of the walls were painted in citrus yellow.

The interiors were being restored at the same time. Some ceilings were restored and several rooms were altered with central arches and new red and green tiles on the floors. Not long before his death in 1759, Gaspare Serenario painted some of the pictures that once decorated the oval ballroom of the *piano nobile*, portraits of the foremost members of the

Right
The monumental double stairway that leads to the *piano nobile*.

Valguarnera family and views of various domains that belonged to them.

In 1760, the painters Pietro Berardi and Giovanni Nicosia undertook the painting in fresco of the stage and the ceiling of the theatre and the dressing room, this last "in the Chinese manner". Pietro Berardi was also commissioned to decorate two rooms of the lower apartment with "figures and flowers in oils", on the walls and the ceilings. The pictures "in this villa", which the Marchese di Villabianca attributed to "the acclaimed painter of birds and flowers Giovan Domenico Osnago, known as Cefalutano" should also be dated to this period.

An engraving by Antonino Bova, which appeared in *Lo Stato Presente della Sicilia*, by Arcangelo Leanti, shows the villa in 1761, surrounded by more or less symmetrical gardens, with the theatrical complex of the drive – restored in the Neoclassical period – a triumphal arch and a circular esplanade with a "labyrinth of water". Even if the documents do not reveal the identity of the creator of this spectacular external arrangement of the villa, recent studies have proposed the names of Giovanni Del Frago, previously mentioned, of Mariano Sucameli, and, in particular, that of the more gifted Andrea Gigante, designer of complicated architectural structures and probable designer, in the 1750s, of the extraordinary pierced wooden ceiling of the hall of

mirrors in the new wing of the Palazzo Valguarnera-Gangi in Palermo, built by the Principe Pietro Valguarnera.

Leanti, in fact, writes that even if the Villa Valguarnera had its beginnings in 1709, it owes its existence mainly to the most noble genius and the cultivated taste of Signore Pietro Valguarnera e Gravina, Principe di Valguarnera, gentleman of the bedchamber, and General of the king of Sardinia. Before, the mountain was a wilderness, and steep too. Yet over time, with masterful artifice and at enormous expense, the area was levelled with tools and underground tunnelling. The result was the magnificent scene that we see today.

Even though Domenico Valguarnera, bishop of Cefalù and brother of Francesco Saverio, had already ordered the enlargement and levelling of the *parterre* in 1740, Pietro modified the terrain around the villa beginning in 1753, seeing to further additions and changes. He altered the drive in the sixties, that is after Bova had made his engraving. The water labyrinth was replaced by storerooms for fruit from the orchards, and in 1767 the marble sculptors Gioacchino and Cosimo Vitagliano and Domenico Gallina were charged with making "a small structure of rough stone with the memorial stone at the centre and a white marble medallion" with a portrait of the Principessa Marianna, Pietro's wife, to be placed in a niche in the drive.

Most of the Neoclassical pictorial decorations of the interiors have recently been attributed to a phase of restoration after the death of Pietro in 1779 and according to the wishes of his wife. The princess was noted for being highly educated although she was a deaf mute; she is delineated in an anonymous description of the villa, dated 1785, as being "unusually gifted in the sciences and the arts" and she came to terms perfectly with the chosen subjects that replaced Pietro's taste for the Rococo. Some of the *saloni* of the *piano nobile* were decorated with themes from mythology. The rooms on the ground floor were dedicated to great men of all periods from antiquity to the eighteenth century, to their discoveries and their achievements: Greek and Roman philosophers and historians (Archimedes and Diodorus), medieval writers (Dante and Petrarch), scientists (Galileo and Newton). Elia Interguglielmi painted the fresco of the *Trionfo del principe illuminato* and the *tondi* with the Labours of Hercules on the ceiling of the circular ballroom on the *piano nobile*. The restorations in the style of Louis XVI on the outside of the villa – which have survived – were entrusted by Marianna and by her son Giuseppe Emanuele to the architect Giovan Battista Cascione and his assistant Vincenzo Fiorelli; they belong to the same cultural climate, by now fully Neoclassical, as the work of Interguglielmi. With the death of Marianna in 1792, and of her architect the previous year, the long period of construction of the villa that heralded the new French Neoclassical taste was finally at an end.

Preceding page
The façade that faces the sea, with the *parterre* that surrounds part of the villa.

Above
The façade and terrace that face the sea.

Opposite
Detail of the decoration of the main façade.

Villa Palagonia in Bagheria

Of those who traveled to Sicily and to Bagheria in the eighteenth century, none could have remained indifferent to the spectacle of the extravagant array of sculpture – alas no longer in its original state – of the avenue, the courtyard and the garden of the villa of the Gravinas, Principi di Palagonia. From impressions noted in travel diaries, of which the authoritative judgments of Goethe take pre-eminence, the critical verdict of two centuries has given us the image of a mad prince; the designer and commissioner of the bizarre exterior and interior decorations of the villa. Perhaps in response to the ironic spirit of a period dedicated to the grotesque and to caricature, the architecture of the villa refers to a line of celebrated and extravagant urban and, more particularly, out-of-town architectural models that date back to the time of Italian Mannerism, and, in particular, to the garden of Bomarzo.

According to the original plans, the villa was to have been surrounded by a *baglio*. This was ordered in about 1715 by Ferdinando Francesco Gravina, Principe di Palagonia and Marchese di Francofonte,

Above
View of the Villa Palagonia with the Porta dei Giganti and the avenue – which no longer exists – in an engraving taken from *Voyage pittoresque des îles de Sicile, de Malte et de Lipari* by Jean P.L.L. Houel (1782–1787).

Opposite
Detail of the convex façade that faces the Villa Valguarnera.

knight of the Golden Fleece and grandee of Spain, who, like the Valguarneras, had leased a tract of land from the Brancifortes. Much in evidence throughout Sicily, he was captain and magistrate of Palermo, first president of the Supreme Council of Sicily and representative of the crown. He underlined his role and his power with ostentatious displays of riches and luxury, with houses splendidly furnished in taste that was continually brought in line with the latest in European avant-garde fashions. For the cream of the aristocracy of Palermo to own a very grand villa in the Bagheria region had, in fact, become obligatory, almost as de rigueur as having a palazzo in town. The founding of the villa was included in a complex program of construction and restoration that also encompassed the property of the Gravinas in Palermo, where the principi lived, as well as the many estates belonging to the family in the eastern part of the island, which had been damaged by the earthquake of 1693. To judge by the documents, it would seem that the plans of the villa should be attributed to Padre Tommaso Maria Napoli; the actual building was then directed by the architect Agostino Daidone. Padre Napoli, a relative of the Principe di Resuttano, had returned from long sojourns in Rome and Vienna and had designed the other main example of Baroque Sicilian architecture, the Villa Valguarnera, a few

years before. The two villas in Bagheria were the fruits of the varied experience he had acquired. According to Erik Neil, he adapted a distinguished model of Roman Mannerism for the country house of the Principe di Palagonia – the pentagonal plan of the Villa Farnese at Caprarola, which had been an essential point of reference for one of the themes proposed on the occasion of the competition held in Rome in 1710 under Pope Clement XI.

Although it may not have enjoyed the same advantageous location as the Villa Valguarnera, the country house of the Palagonia family could originally boast a slightly elevated position; it had two original entrances, formed where the road that still cuts through the ground floor pierced the external walls, and consequently two main façades. On one of these, the convex façade that is turned towards the Villa Valguarnera, the pentagonal plan permitted an interesting movement of angular projections; to this was added, on the *piano nobile*, the play of masses and voids created by the presence of two terraces that flank a closed central loggia. The spectacular complex double staircase forms the central element of the opposite concave façade, which became the main façade when the avenue and the Porta dei Giganti were added in the second half of the century. In 1718, the villa should have been finished; Procopio Serpotta, son of the

Below
The porta dei Giganti once provided access to the avenue that led up to the villa.

Opposite
One of the two terraces that flank the closed loggia on the façade that is turned towards the Villa Valguarnera.

Following pages
The monumental double staircase leading to the *piano nobile*.

better-known Giacomo, had been engaged to do the stucco decoration for the interiors. But the original plan that Ferdinando Francesco Gravina and Tommaso Maria Napoli wanted to carry out was changed by successive owners.

From 1741 to 1745, while work was being carried out in the Palazzo in Via Alloro into which the Gravinas had just moved, the new prince, Ignazio Sebastiano, entrusted the construction of several buildings of the *baglio* that surrounds the villa to the architect Nicolò Troisi, who came from Trapani. These included a chapel and a row of low buildings to be used as stables and storerooms. The work continued even after the death of the prince in 1746, by the order of his son, Ferdinando Francesco. The work of Francesco Ferrigno, architect to the senate of Palermo, was short and of little significance, whereas more commitment was shown, according to the documents discovered by Neil, in the achievements of Rosario L'Avocato, the prince's own architect. The work of L'Avocato, documented at Villa Palagonia from 1751 to 1772, brought the construction of the service buildings to a conclusion and also entailed restoration and modernization of the villa itself. The same architect was probably responsible for the inlayed marble paving, dated 1758, in the covered loggia, and for the conception of the garden and of the avenue, both characterized by the presence of numerous statues in tufa representing people of all sorts. Heroic and mythological figures, animals, peasants and musicians, women and soldiers, dwarfs, monsters and beings half-human and half-animal were once united in a long tableau along the avenue and along the wall that surrounded the villa, or scattered individually all over the garden. This has been revealed by sources and via the evidence, in graphic form, of two engravings of the 1770s and 1780s – published respectively in the *Voyage pittoresque des îles de Sicile, de Malte et de Lipari* by Jean Houel and in the *Lettres sur la Sicile et sur île de Malte* by Michel Jean, Compte de Borch, to which should be added a sketch by Louis Ducros.

A document from 1753 is the only significant source with the names of the sculptors who worked at the Villa Palagonia, although this source does not refer to the so-called monsters. The marble workers Agostino Vitagliano, Carmelo Rizzo, Giuseppe Muscarello and Filippo di Stefano were commissioned to devise two fountains, of which one —no longer extant – was decorated with putti, griffins, gargoyles and statues, after a design by Rosario L'Avocato.

It is now difficult to identify the allegorical sources of the "monsters", and thus to interpret the narrative intent of the groups. Some scholars have proposed analogies with the iconography of sixteenth-

century northern pictorial works. A comparison with contemporary Meissen porcelain figures, as suggested by Gioacchino Lanza Tomasi, would be more precise; the only accurate reference is to the musicians, who undoubtedly derive from the engravings in the *Gabinetto armonico, pieno d'istromenti sonori, indicati, spiegati e di nuovo corretti ed accresciuti dal padre Filippo Bonanno della Compagnia di Gesù* (Collection of musical instruments, labeled, explained and expounded upon by the Jesuit Father Filippo Bonanno).

Indeed, even contemporaries found it impossible to interpret these scenes. Jean Houel, on a visit to Villa Palagonia in 1777, indicated a general derivation of the subjects of the groups "from stories, fables or romances, or else from scenes of fashionable society". During the last years of the younger Ferdinando Francesco, more precisely on 9 April 1787, Goethe visited Bagheria; although his description of the villa of the Gravinas is pervaded with disappointment, it can nonetheless be used to reconstruct an idea of its bizarre appearance. A lover of the order and clarity of the classical world, champion of the ideal of beauty, he noted with disgust in his travel diary how the many roughly-hewn figures that constitute the strange groups of the avenue had sprung into being without sense or understanding and had been jumbled together indiscriminately and without

an objective, thus denying any narrative intent. Around the house, scattered in confusion on ground almost completely covered in grass, as though in a neglected churchyard, lay marble vases adorned with strange volutes, dwarfs and monsters lying face down. A wooden crucifix was fixed horizontally to the vaulting of the chapel, with a chain hanging from its navel; from this chain dangled the head of a penitent. The peculiarities continued inside the house, itself arranged according to an anomalous plan, where "The legs of the chairs are sawn off at unequal lengths ... the velvet upholstery conceals sharp prickles ...". There were what appeared to be Chinese porcelain candelabra, actually made of diverse dishes, cups and saucers, and other objects haphazardly stuck together, while the stained glass windows distorted "... the enchanting view of the promontories ...". Goethe also refers to "a large, sumptuously and colorfully decorated room started by the father [of the younger prince Ferdinando Francesco] ... which remained unfinished".

This is undoubtedly the renowned ballroom whose ceiling was covered in mirrors as early as 1770, when visited by Patrick Brydone. According to Brydone's description, there were other rooms with this type of decoration, which even extended to doors covered in "small mirrors cut in the most ridiculous shapes and interspersed with glass

and crystal of every kind and color". Work was still continuing in the ballroom when Jean Houel described it more accurately in 1777: a false cornice – still visible today – ran around the lower edge of the ceiling, painted with architectural motifs, Rococo volutes, and fantastic animals. The walls were "decorated with large medallions, placed between pilasters; the background [of the walls] appears to be of jasper or marble, but consists only of pieces of clear glass painted to look like jasper or marble". The significance of these mirrors that repeated to infinity the image of whoever passed beneath them is explained by the text placed above the door that leads into the reception rooms: "Gaze into these mirrors, and in that same singular resplendence, contemplate the mortal frailty of the image they bring forth."

The inventory compiled on the death of Ferdinando Francesco in 1788 is of great interest for an understanding of the state of the villa at that time. The inventory confirms that the mirror decoration extended to various rooms adjacent to the ballroom – now decorated with Neo-classical pictures in imitation of those at Pompeii – and attests to the presence of furnishings that were sumptuous in the extreme. Fifty-four paintings were hung in the oval entrance hall and it thus seems certain that the present wall paintings that depict the *The Labours of*

Hercules among landscapes and illusionist architecture were commissioned by the subsequent owner, as were the decorations of the private rooms to the left of the entrance hall. These have ceilings painted with grotesques, with panels that enclose arcadian scenes and scenes

from mythology, stories taken from *Orlando Furioso*, ancient temples, and landscapes. As the inventory testifies that these rooms were covered in brocade, 1788 also became the *terminus post quem* for the

Above
The mirrored ballroom with walls of imitation marble and medallions containing marble busts. The reflections of people and objects in the myriads of mirrors on the ceiling continued to infinity, alluding to the transience of earthly things.

dating of the exotic scenes painted on the walls of the alcove and signed by Aniello Sgaraglia, an almost unknown artist of uncertain Neapolitan provenance. These paintings portray an oriental city where, among lively scenes of daily life, horsemen and musicians in procession accompany a personage in a sedan chair, while elsewhere there is a parade of finely caparisoned horses.

According to the reports of the times, immediately after the death of Ferdinando Francesco, Salvatore Gravina – the prince's stepbrother and successor, having married his only daughter and heir – saw to the removal of a few statues from the garden. This was the first, symbolic show of force against the old, eighteenth-century culture and that of the Baroque, and it rode the wave that was precipitating a new sensibility. The major building work at the Villa Palagonia ended definitively with a new phase of restoration that was the natural continuation of that gesture. An account signed by the architect Luigi Del Frago in 1794 concerns work of secondary importance, but which is nonetheless indicative of the fact that the decorations of the interiors were, at the time, being modernized to conform with the new taste for the Neoclassical.

Palazzo Valguarnera-Gangi in Palermo

Palazzo Valguarnera-Gangi, one of the most important houses of Sicily, is located in the heart of the Kalsa quarter, in an area filled with imposing aristocratic residences. Its fame derives from its immeasurable artistic value. The present appearance of the palace dates from the refurbishment of an earlier building, begun in the second half of the eighteenth century by Don Pietro Valguarnera. Around 1748 Valguarnera married his niece, Marianna. She was the protagonist of one of the novels of Dacia Maraini and the eldest daughter and heir of Francesco Saverio, Principe di Valguarnera. As the prince died without a male successor, Valguarnera acquired both titles and property, including the palace in the city and the villa at Bagheria, both of which he set about refurbishing immediately after the wedding. In 1770 Pietro and Marianna regained the title of Principe di Gangi, which the Valguarnera family had held since 1660 but which the guardians of Marianna had temporarily conferred on Ruggero Settimo, Marchese di Giarratana.

The commencement of work at Palazzo Valguarnera-

Above
One of the façades of Palazzo Valguarnera-Gangi.

Below
The façade on Piazza dei Vespri.
The main entrance leads into the
inner courtyard.

Gangi may be seen as part of a general refurbishment of the city's buildings in the second half of the eighteenth century. Though this probably began in response to the damage caused by the earthquake of 1751, it soon developed into a kind of contest in which prominent members of the aristocracy attempted to outdo each other in displays of magnificence.

As Erik Neil has shown, little is known about the appearance of the building prior to the works documented from 1754. The works became more frequent after 1757, when documents first record the presence of Andrea Gigante. He was a young architect from Trapani, who had recently arrived in the capital and was employed in a major refurbishment project

Above and right
The Galleria degli Specchi (Gallery of the Mirrors), with its perforated wooden ceiling, is situated in the new wing of the palace, designed by the architect Andrea Gigante from 1757.

Left
A corner of the Galleria degli
Specchi (Gallery of the Mirrors).
The carving of the *boiserie*, in
"Venetian" style, was
commissioned from Giuseppe
Melia and Giovanni Battista Rizzo
in the late 1750s.

Opposite
One of the two *poudreuses*
decorated in Chinese style,
situated beyond the rear wall of
the Galleria degli Specchi.

at the palace and, in particular, in the construction of a
new wing overlooking Piazza
dei Vespri and containing the
remarkable Galleria degli
Specchi (Gallery of the
Mirrors). A masterpiece of the
Sicilian Baroque, the Galleria
had a spectacular perforated
double ceiling, the conception
of which should probably be
attributed to Gigante. The
design, similar to the work of
artists such as Andrea Pozzo
and the Bibienas, is likely to
have been inspired by contact
with the architect Giovanni
Biagio Amico, with whom

Gigante trained in Trapani. Amico's interest in complex designs of striking dramatic effect – in particular, in perforated double-shell ceilings – is documented by his work as a theorist and writer of treatises.

Gigante's work at Palazzo Valguarnera and the contemporaneous construction of the grand staircase in Palazzo Bonagia in Via Alloro – undertaken when he was aged about 25 – showed that he had absorbed the lessons of Amico before veering towards a Neoclassical style. This was perhaps as a consequence of the return of the Sicilian Neoclassical artist par excellence,

Giuseppe Venanzio Marvuglia from Rome in the early 1760s. Gigante was thus, at the beginning of his career, an early exponent in Sicily of the Rococo style that was currently fashionable at the courts of Europe, and also, in those same years, becoming popular in Naples. Between 1757 and 1758, he began work on the decoration of the Salone da Ballo (Ballroom), the Galleria, and a number of small rooms known as *poudreuses*. Pietro Valguarnera supplied the artists Giuseppe Melia and Giovanni Battista Rizzo with designs in the so-called "Venetian" style for the carving in these rooms – specifically, of windows, doors, ornaments and sopraporta (overdoor) panels.

Gaspare Serenario, who also worked at the family villa at Bagheria sometime before 1759, the year of his death, and who was responsible for the fresco on the ceiling of the Salone da Ballo depicting the *Triumph of Faith*, was commissioned to provide a number of designs for the painted decoration, which were then executed by Pietro Berardi on the carved wood, on the stuccowork, and on the walls of numerous rooms, including several in Chinese style. Serenario may also be responsible for the decoration of the perforated ceiling of the Galleria degli Specchi, which is painted with imitation volutes, putti, shells and bouquets.

From 1759 to 1764 documents record the presence of another architect in the

Opposite
The monumental staircase and the second-floor entrance gallery.

Below
The terrace attributed by the records to the architect Mariano Sucameli.

palace workshop, Mariano Sucameli. He produced new works in the style established by Gigante, including the terrace, the grand staircase, the courtyard, and the decoration of the outside of the house with statues, vases, medallions and cornices. In the same period, Pietro Valguarnera commissioned the magnificent maiolica floors, which depict, in the Galleria, the *Labours of Hercules*, and, in the Salone da Ballo, *Battle Scenes*. Records show that Pietro also took an interest in the palace furnishings, some of which still survive. In a perfect stylistic synthesis, the whole decorative appearance was made to mirror the themes of its structural surroundings, in such a way creating an outstanding example of late-Baroque architecture.

Little remains of the work of Sucameli. Indeed, the palace was soon to be radically altered as a result of works commissioned in the 1780s by the new Principe di Gangi, Giuseppe Emanuele Valguarnera. These alterations have been attributed to the architect Giovan Battista Cascione, whose name appears in several documents in relation to works completed between 1780 and 1785. The elegant two-flight staircase that still exists and the remodelling of the exterior, inspired by the new Neo-classical style, may be ascribed to Cascione.

The paintings of several rooms date from the end of the eighteenth century or the early years of the nineteenth.

Below
The Salone Ovale (Oval Room). In the central panel of the vault, the painting shows *Psyche Led to Olympus by Mercury*. It is attributed to Giuseppe Velasco.

Opposite
A wall of the Salone Ovale, with the coat of arms of the princes of Valguarnera painted on the floor in maiolica.

These include the succession of green, red and blue rooms that contain a number of extremely valuable collections – porcelain from the principal European manufacturers from Sèvres to Meissen, *biscuit* from Vienna and Capodimonte, glass from Murano, lace, and fans. According to the records available, some of these paintings – which include both frescoes and oils on canvas – would have been produced by Giuseppe Velasco, the major exponent of Sicilian Neoclassical painting. This is quite likely to be true of the decoration of the vaulted ceiling of the Salone Ovale (Oval Room), the central panel of which depicts *Psyche Led to Olympus by Mercury*, over whose authorship scholars are agreed, while the attribution to Velasco of the *Mythological Figures* above the doors of several rooms remains doubtful. Indeed, a document of 1781 records that the painter and scenographer Giuseppe Fiorenza received payment for a "painted decoration depicting Daphne pursued by Apollo," which may perhaps be identified with one of these mythological paintings. During the same years Eugenio Fumagalli was remunerated for various unspecified paintings, while Elia Interguglielmi signed and dated in 1792 the fresco on the vaulted ceiling of the princes' bedroom, depicting *Mars Presents the Prince to Jupiter*.

This was probably one of the last works to be executed before the title of Principe di Gangi passed to another

prominent Sicilian aristocratic family with the marriage, in 1804, of Agata Valguarnera, the last descendant of the family, to Giuseppe Alliata, Principe di Villafranca. It was later ceded, with the palace itself, to the Mantegna family. Later still, this magnificent house was acquired by the

Vanni Calvello family, to whom it still belongs.

Across the centuries the palace has had a number of distinguished guests. As well as several of the principal

European royal families, it has accommodated artists such as the Belgian painter van Broesick, and composers such as Gioacchino Rossini and Vincenzo Bellini. Richard Wagner, who according to family anecdotes began to compose *Parsifal* in the rooms of the palace, left the prince a letter of farewell, in which he remarked, "I cannot leave Sicily, dear Prince, without expressing my thanks and assuring you that I take with me the most precious memories of your goodness and of Palazzo Gangi."

Below and opposite
Rooms in the palace.

Palazzo Biscari in Catania

On 3 May 1787, Johann Wolfgang Goethe, who was passing through Catania, was received at the Principe di Biscari's palace.

As might be imagined, the Baroque architectural style of this noble residence did not excite admiration from the Frankfurt writer, who greatly revered the classical world. He made no comment on the palace. But what did strike Goethe was the richness of the collections of antiquities which filled the apartments. He noted: "And I have learnt something more, allowing myself, with some profit, to be led by the unbroken thread of Winckelmann, which guides us through the various periods of art."

The Comte De Borch had little to add in his *Lettres sur la Sicile et sur l'île de Malthe*, published in 1782, though written five years earlier, remarking that "Si son extérieur n'affiche pas beaucoup de magnificence, l'intérieur compense bien ce défaut par les beautés qu'il renferme (Though the exterior may not be particularly splendid, the interior makes up for it with all the beauties it contains)."

The earliest reference to the building dates from 1695, shortly before the demolition

Above
A corner of the main courtyard of the palace, with the staircase that leads into the reception room.

Opposite
The terrace of the façade overlooking the sea, with the famous decorated windows that were commissioned from the sculptor Antonino Amato of Messina (from 1707)

of a palace belonging to the Paternò Castello family, Principi di Biscari. This palace occupied approximately the same area as the present-day palace but did not rise above the city walls. It also suffered extensive damage in the disastrous earthquake of 1693. Almost nothing in Catania was spared, and the day after the tragedy, the Viceroy of Uzeda took the decision to rebuild the city, making use of the old city walls which had partly survived.

Only a few, privileged, aristocratic families obtained permission to build their own houses on the walls, among them the Principi di Biscari, who became the owners of the most important palace in the city. Documents affirm that a continuous and systematic series of works relating to the construction of the new house began in 1702, at the instigation of the seventeen-year-old Vincenzo, who had recently become the fourth Principe di Biscari, and who the following year "began to rebuild his property in a magnificent fashion and bought various houses so as to enhance and embellish this city."

One document of 1707 records a commission to Antonino Amato of Messina for "seven windows of carved white stone … for the façade overlooking the sea", which extends along two sides of the building, and for two other windows of a different design for the main courtyard. The doors of the façade overlooking the sea, which, noted

Below and opposite
The decoration of the Galleria degli Uccelli (Gallery of the Birds) was completed around 1766, with the purchase of the maiolica floor tiles from Naples and the oriental porcelain for the console tables. The furniture of the Galleria is also from the eighteenth century.

Anthony Blunt, exploded in a luxuriant fantasy of carved scrolls, putti and garlands, were framed by pilasters, also richly carved, in which two old men hold up ornamental panels above which a telamon supports the capital. The building which surrounds the main courtyard must therefore have existed at that time. Several documents, dating from the first decade of the century onwards, suggest that the architect Alonzo di Benedetto of Catania may have been responsible for its design and supervised its construction. Before 1731 the four large rooms of the house, corresponding to the doors on the same façade, were completed with stuccowork and gilding.

A new series of works begun in 1739 were occasioned by the imminent wedding of Ignazio, the eldest son of Vincenzo. The works were also inspired by the rise of more modern architectural trends brought to Catania from Rome by Giovan Battista Vaccarini, who had for some time been "Architect Commissioner Prefect for Works in the City." The engineer Giuseppe Palazzotto was entrusted with the task of producing a design in keeping with the new styles, which was executed between 1743 and 1764. It provided for the decoration of a number of rooms, the alteration and completion of the external façades and those on the courtyard, and the construction of a new wing to the east

of the palace, which would accommodate an apartment for the new couple.

Vincenzo died in 1744. The new principe, Ignazio, was a man of considerable culture. Having come into contact with intellectuals of European renown on his many travels, he was a connoisseur of music and the theater, a collector of art and antiquities, and a promoter of excavations in and around Catania.

Palazzotto was succeeded after his death in 1764 by the architect Francesco Battaglia, who designed a new wing to the southeast of the original building, completed around 1766. The classical character of the exterior and the elegance of a number of private rooms in the southern apartment may be attributed to the partnership of Battaglia and Principe Ignazio, who was himself an architect. The extension of the façade overlooking the sea, which corresponds to the Galleria (Gallery) built onto the large Salone da Ballo (Ballroom), in fact dates from 1764–1765. The façade displays a classical arrangement, with three, tall, round-arched windows flanked by pairs of columns and pilaster strips, and topped by trabeation resting on capitals.

According to the records, the following year witnessed the decoration of a number of rooms, most probably intended for private use, in the new wing, including the remarkable Galleria degli Uccelli (Gallery of the Birds) and

Below
One of the wooden panels in the Galleria degli Uccelli (Gallery of the Birds) that are painted with a vast ornithological repertoire.

Opposite
The Stanza di Don Chisciotte (Room of Don Quixote) — also known as the Stanza di Conversazione (Conversation Room) — which takes its name from the stories depicted in the oil-paintings on the walls.

the Stanza di Don Chisciotte (Room of Don Quixote). These rooms constitute one of the most refined examples of chinoiserie in the whole of Sicily. The first has a vaulted ceiling decorated with stucco-work, with fine, gilded mouldings framing oriental scenes depicted in relief. Along the walls, mirrors and console tables alternate with doors and panels painted with birds of every species, all shown in their natural habitat. A number of documents from 1766 record the purchase in Naples of ceramic tiles and Japanese porcelain, of "porcelain statues from the Indies," "from China, and from the factory in Paris, in the latest fashion," to be arranged on the numerous console tables of the Galleria. The same date is engraved in the stucco that decorates the vaulted ceiling of the Stanza di Don Chisciotte, also known as the Stanza di Conversazione (Conversation Room), where the ornithological repertoire – yet another of the interests of the eclectic Principe Ignazio – continues. In addition to these fixed paintings the room contains a series of canvases depicting *Stories from Don Quixote*, which have been tentatively attributed to Sebastiano Lo Monaco. The source for these paintings is a series of designs by Charles-Antoine Coypel that were used in the production of the tapestries made by Gobelins for the King of France. These designs circulated widely in Europe as engravings to an

edition of Cervantes that was published in 1744, a copy of which is listed in the Biscari hereditary inventories from the end of the eighteenth century.

Numerous payments to an array of artists and artisans for the decoration of rooms are recorded from 1769 to the

Below
The Salone da Ballo (Ballroom), with the alcove at the end of the room. The room's elaborate decorative scheme was probably completed by 1772.

1780s. Among them, the name of Antonio Emmanuele, nicknamed "Pepe", recurs, as being the person responsible for decoration and furniture. The decoration of the Salone da Ballo, described by Blunt as the most flowing example of

Opposite
The vaulted ceiling of the Salone da Ballo, the frescoes of which were probably painted by Matteo Desiderato and Sebastiano Lo Monaco. The central opening, around which the orchestra was positioned, is covered with a frescoed cupola depicting *The Glory of the Biscari Family*

Rococo decoration known in Sicily, was probably completed by 1772, the year in which the young Vincenzo married. One of the small landscapes painted above the doors of the Salone is dated 1771 and signed by the Neapolitan Eustachio Pessi, while the floor tiles for this room and those next to it were ordered from Naples in the same year.

Shaped like an elongated octagon, the Salone da Ballo has an elaborate decorative scheme, with an alcove at the back of the room, fireplaces in the corner niches, console tables and mirrors. During the early 1780s, Matteo Desiderato and Sebastiano Lo Monaco – who was probably Desiderato's pupil – were entrusted with the frescoes of a number of rooms, including those within the stucco mouldings of the vaulted ceiling of the Salone da Ballo. Desiderato is generally attributed with the allegorical figures of the lower panels, and Lo Monaco with *The Glory of the Biscari Family* painted on the cupola above the opening at the centre of the ceiling, where a balustraded gallery accommodated the orchestra.

It is likely that the collaboration between Battaglia and the master decorators and stucco-workers also gave rise to the exquisite staircase that leads to the orchestra gallery. It is situated at the end of the narrow gallery that separates the Salone da Ballo from the windows of the façade and its vaulted ceiling is decorated

with frescoes attributed to Lo Monaco. The stuccowork of this ceiling and that of the Salone – which is believed to be the work of Gioacchino Gianforma and Ignazio Mazzeo, who collaborated with Lo Monaco on a number of projects in eastern Sicily – perhaps shows the influence

Below and opposite
The staircase decorated with stucco leads to the orchestra gallery, which is situated above the Salone da Ballo (Ballroom).

of the French Rocaille engravings that were very popular at the time, while, as Blunt points out, the technique is similar to that used in certain Bavarian and Venetian works of the eighteenth century.

The garden of the western courtyard, with its series of four pavilions with pagoda roofs, probably dates from the 1780s.

In order to satisfy the cultural interests of the principe, Battaglia also designed the Biscari theater and undertook the construction of a new museum. An earlier project to install a museum next to the house using designs by Palazzotto had begun between 1752 and 1757. It consisted of large rooms arranged around two new courtyards and held the prince's ever-growing collections of antiquities and objects of natural historical interest. Battaglia is certainly responsible for the balanced and soberly elegant character of the two-coloured exterior of the museum and of its interior, work on which continued up to 1785.

A number of further alterations were made after the death of Battaglia and the arrival of his son, Antonino, in 1788. These included the partial rearrangement of the main courtyard, the incorporation into the palace of a neighbouring group of houses, previously the property of the Barone di Raddusa, and the construction of the stables and of the entrance on the piazza.

Palazzo Comitini in Palermo

In *Palermo Today*, the Marchese di Villabianca noted that Salvatore Gravina e Gravina, Principe di Comitini, owned a palace with a first and second courtyard, marble colonnades, and truly magnificent apartments, in Corso della Strada Nuova, in the Albergaria quarter, on the corner of Strada del Bosco. It was built in recent times by the late Principe Giuseppe Gravina, *Expretor* of Palermo. Part of this palace was the house of the Principi di Roccafiorita Bonanni. In its earliest form, the palace, which then belonged to the Bonanno family, princes of Roccafiorita, fronted on Via del Bosco. Its original appearance, with two floors and a main door with a polygonal arch, is preserved in an engraving in *La Reggia in trionfo per l'acclamazione della Sacra Real Maestà di Carlo Infante di Spagna* (The Palace in Triumph for the Acclamation of His Royal Highness Charles, Infante of Spain) by Pietro La Placa, which shows the palace festively decorated for the entrance of Charles III into Palermo in 1735. The house then passed, possibly through marriage, to a secondary branch of the Gravina family, on whom

Charles II had conferred the title of "Principi di Comitini e Santa Maria d'Altomonte" in 1673. The refurbishment and enlargement of the old building most probably started in 1766, the date that appears on the frame of one of the windows of the courtyard close to Via del Bosco. The refurbishment was at the instigation of Michele Gravina e Gravina, Principe di Comitini, Magistrate of Palermo, Governor of the Company of the Bianchi, and Deputy of the Kingdom, who wanted his house to have a suitably grand façade on Strada Nova, also called Strada Maqueda. This road formed a new axis within the city walls and it greatly altered the medieval layout of the city. Until then, the city had been based around the Cassaro, the ancient Strada Marmorea which began at the Porta Nuova near Palazzo Reale; in the second half of the sixteenth century, it was straightened and extended to the coast.

Leonardo Sciascia, in the introduction to *Palermo Felicissima* (Most Happy Palermo), wrote of Rosario La Duca: "This gate-city, this straight-road city, this non-city city, was not to the liking of Don Bernardino Cardines, Duca di Maqueda, who was Viceroy of Sicily from 1 April 1598 to 16 December 1601 … So [and here he quotes the chronicler Vincenzo Auria], "he built a new road which he called Macheda, after his dukedom, similar to the Cassaro, the two of them

forming a long cross, by which sacred, holy sign the city was perpetually guarded. Palermo was thus divided into four parts, commonly called quarters: each constitutes a separate city. Strada Macheda was opened for the first time on 24 July 1600, inaugurated by the Viceroy himself, who

Preceding pages
The gallery and the arches of the gallery leading into the *piano nobile*.

made the first blow on the first stone with a silver hammer. The road begins at the gate which is itself called the Porta Macheda, and finishes at the Porta dei Vicari." Along this new axis several prominent aristocratic families built their own houses, among them the Principi Filangeri di Cutò, the Costantinos, the Rudinìs, and the Celestris, Marchesi di

Above and opposite
The entrance hall of the *piano nobile*, its ceiling and walls covered with *trompe l'œil* architectural perspectives.

Santa Croce. The *Diari* (Diaries) of the Marchese di Villabianca contain the following passage: "The year 1768 finally saw the completion of the construction of the magnificent palace of Michele Gravina Crujllas, Principe di Comitini, *Expretor* of Palermo, which stands on Strada Maqueda, commonly known as Strada Nuova, a palace which has six different areas, a courtyard with double columns in the middle, and altogether radiates magnificence. It lacked only the ennoblement of the façade, which, at that point, still had a rustic character and eleven windows. The façade was finally finished in 1771, with many adornments and with four columns of grey marble placed by the two entrances." The design for the enlargement of Palazzo Comitini has traditionally been attributed to Nicolò Palma, Senate architect from 1730. The name of Orazio Furetto has also been proposed, to whom there are references in a number of reliable sources, while recent studies tend to favour Giovan Battista Cascione, the son of a painter of *trompe l'œil* perspectives who trained in the circle of the architect Giovan Battista Vaccarini, his uncle.

Cascione, who was active from the 1750s, was responsible for the Palermitan palace of the Principi di Villafranca in Piazza Bologni. Like this building, Palazzo Comitini has two entrances, and a grand staircase in the main courtyard. It has an irregular trapezoidal form and was originally on two floors, which became three in 1931 with the resulting destruction of the cornice and the attic. On the second floor, or *piano nobile*, majestic balconies with triangular and curved tympanums alternate, decorated with motifs of curls and garlands. There are three windows above the two entrances, joined by a single, goose-neck, wrought-iron railings, the larger, central window having a broken curved tympanum.

The two main doors are both flanked by two Billiemi

Below
The Salone Rosso (Red Room), one of the reception rooms of the palace.

Opposite
The panel above the door of the Salone Verde (Green Room), painted with a *Scene with Putti Playing*, attributed to Elia Interguglielmi.

columns resting on high plinths and crowned with the coat of arms of the Gravina family. The one on the left leads into the main courtyard, which is divided into two areas by a gallery with three arches. At the bottom is the grand staircase, its depressed arch framed by columns and trabeation. The staircase, made of Ogliastro marble, leads to the gallery with three arches and a limestone balustrade. The semicircular end wall of the balustrade contains a fountain, consisting of a shell surmounted with a putto riding a dolphin.

The gallery gives access to the entrance hall of the *piano nobile*; at one time its floor was covered with maiolica bricks made by the Neapolitan firm Attanasio. The room is characterized by perspective decoration which completely covers both the ceiling, which shows a row of balconies held up by corbels and adorned with vases of flowers, and also the walls, where country scenes appear beyond a curtain and an arcade.

The reception rooms follow on from the block which divides the courtyard. The first – the Salone Verde (Green Room) – has a stucco ceiling, and above-door panels painted with playful putti, which Maria Accascina has attributed to Elia Interguglielmi. The two portraits of the Duchi di Reitano in the neighbouring Salone Rosso (Red Room) have been ascribed to the same artist. To the left of the Salone Rosso is the Salone degli Specchi (Room of the Mirrors), which is also known as the Sala Martorana, after the painter of the frescoes on the ceiling, Gioacchino Martorana, one of the most representative artists of the period. The fresco at the center of the ceiling depicts the *Triumph of Love*, and those

Below and opposite
Details of the decoration of one of the two *boudoirs* next to the princes' bedroom.

of the corner medallions the *Four Cardinal Virtues*. Gilded stuccowork of rocaille motifs fills the spaces between the pictures and frames *Scenes with Putti* and *Seascapes*. The room, richly decorated with *boiserie*, is distinguished by a collection of canvases by southern Italian artists of the seventeenth century, placed above the doors, while a series of landscapes is set in above the mirrors. On the other side of

the entrance hall two small rooms give access to the princes' bedroom, which has a stucco ceiling and still retains part of the original furnishings. Next to this room are two small *boudoirs* entirely decorated with plant motifs in gilded stucco, alternating with corbels and maiolica discs of various sizes from the Florio factory. These replaced the original discs at the beginning of the twentieth century. A collection of leaded mirrors from Murano, on which silver reliefs depict Arcadian scenes, concludes the decoration of these exquisite private rooms; on the ceilings, the stuccowork is more dense, framing painted architectural structures with floral motifs.

In 1926 the palace was acquired by the provincial administration, which still has its seat in the magnificent residence of the principi di Comitini.

Below
The Salone degli Specchi (Room of Mirrors) has seventeenth-century paintings above the doors, and stuccowork and frescoes by Gioacchino Martorana on the ceiling.

Opposite
Fortitude, one of the *Four Cardinal Virtues* painted in one of the corner medallions of the ceiling of the Salone degli Specchi.

Villa Camastra-Tasca in Palermo

In a chapter dedicated to the *Contrade rusticane e littorali* (Rural and coastal districts) of Palermo, the Marchese di Villabianca has the following to say of Mezzo Monreale: "This district is so called because it is situated halfway between Palermo and the city of Monreale. Its ancient road, which runs for over two miles in a straight line from Porta Nuova to Monreale, could be called the new, greater Cassaro, being more noble than the Cassaro itself. It is wider, and consists almost entirely of magnificent palaces and noble buildings on both sides, interspersed with open spaces and public fountains, which create the impression of an urban area, rather than a suburban road lined with poplars. The surrounding countryside was adorned with noble villas and delightful houses, with gardens everywhere, enriched with springs and streams." Positioned along the road of Mezzo Monreale "is a large open space, which is used as a training ground by the army. It is called 'Camastra' because it belongs to the Duca di Camastra, Giuseppe Lanza, or, rather, to his heir, the Principe di Trabia." The suburban residence which

Opposite
The main façade of Villa Camastra-Tasca.

belonged to the duchi di Camastra in the second half of the eighteenth century was originally one of the garden-villas commissioned between the end of the sixteenth century and the early years of the seventeenth by Ercole Branciforte, Duca di San Giovanni, and his wife Agata, who belonged to one of the most powerful families in Sicily. According to the scholar Nino Basile, it was built on the site of an earlier villa – marked by the number 114 on the topographical map of Palermo produced by Matteo Florimi in the second half of the sixteenth century.

The villa was built around 1559 by Don Aloisio Beccadelli of Bologna, Barone di Montefranco, as testified by a fragment of a marble escutcheon which adorned a wall of an ancient building next to today's Villa Tasca. It is likely that the villa was then inherited by Beccadelli's fifth daughter, Maria, the wife of Ludovico Comes de Silvera, who was a Magistrate of Palermo in 1584, then Harbour Master, and eventually Royal Keeper of the Kingdom. Indeed, during the following centuries the Camastra residence was also known by the name Silvera.

According to a number of documents drawn up in 1642 in relation to a hereditary lawsuit between Francesco Branciforte, Duca di San Giovanni, and Antonio Branciforte, Principe di Scordia, the nephew and the son of Ercole Branciforte, respectively, Donna Agata Branciforte e Lanza, Ercole's wife, had bought a garden lying on the Monreale road, which formerly belonged to the late Mariano di Paci, and in which the said Donna Agata, with her own money, did many good works and made many improvements and adornments, with many fountains and other delights, all at her own expense. The same documents record that the Illustrious Don Ercole, during his lifetime, removed all the marble statues – some of them Roman – from the garden of a villa he had built slightly earlier, between the late 1580s and early 1590s, in

the village of San Michele, near Cammarata, in the province of Agrigento. He then installed the statues "in a garden made by the late Illustrious Don Ercole in the territory of this city of Palermo, on the road to Monreale. The garden-villa of San Michele no longer

exists, but a detailed description of it was published in 1642 by Ercole's son, Ottavio. Along an intricate pathway, this wonderful garden, full of statues and fountains, grottoes, labyrinths and ornamental waterworks, purified the spirit, and, liberating it from the passions, led it towards the villa, where an inscription above the main entrance read: "Built by Ercole Branciforte, for the honest repose of himself, his family, and his friends."

Nothing remains of the Villa Branciforte at Camastra. It may nevertheless be assumed that the neostoic atmosphere which emanates from Ottavio's description of the villa at San Michele also permeated the house at Camastra. Its delights are described by Francesco Baronio, in his *De majestate panormitana* (On the Grandeur of Palermo), published in 1630. The garden was adorned with fountains and statues, while unexpected jets of water punished those who dared to look into a mirror suspended on a wall of the house and hidden by leaves – a curiosity that was also found at the villa at San Michele. In the eighteenth century, the villa at Mezzo Monreale belonged to the Lanza family, Principi di Trabia and Duchi di Camastra. Towards the end of the century, it was described, with other suburban residences, by the Marchese di Villabianca. The villa, "a noble palace, flanked

by two towers, with delightful gardens, is situated in the district called Silvera. In the past, it was one of the finest villas owned by our barons, and the present princes of Trabia, to whom it now belongs, have with noble talent extended the gardens and the delightful walks."

During that period the Lanza family was engaged in reorganizing the garden in front of the villa into geometric beds – in place of the earlier garden of the Brancifortes – and in modernizing the design of the house, still seventeenth-century in character, in accordance with the new Neoclassical style. A number of alterations were made by the architect Andrea Gigante from Trapani, who, after a youthful phase in which he fully took on the late-Baroque style, turned his attention to the classicism of Giuseppe Venanzio Marvuglia, who had returned from Rome in the early 1760s. A tempera painting from the end of the eighteenth century and an oil-painting from the first half of the nineteenth record the appearance of Villa Camastra during that period – a Neoclassical façade, with a classical pediment in the center and an external staircase with an ascent on either side. The two embattled side-towers, which no longer survive, may, according to Gioacchino Lanza Tomasi, have formed part of the seventeenth-century building. Gigante was also responsible for the reorganization of the interior of the house, where

the decoration of the ceilings and walls with classical landscapes, ruins and statues has been attributed to the Neapolitan painter Benedetto Cotardi. He was described as "an extremely skilful perspective painter and a decorator of great merit." The attribution to Cotardi is supported by the fact that the painter was working with Gigante at Villa Galletti-Inguaggiato at Bagheria in the same period, where he executed architectural perspectives of great scenic effect, using designs and cartoons, according to Maria Giuffré, by Gigante. The magnificent maiolica

Preceding pages
One of the architectural perspectives painted on the ceiling of one of the rooms.

Below and opposite
Two corners of a room. *Landscapes with Classical Architecture* are depicted between cornices on the walls. The maiolica floor was produced in Naples.

floors of Villa Camastra, signed by the Neapolitan Attanasio and dated 1777, set a precise date on the conclusion of the works by Gigante. When in 1840 Beatrice Lanza e Branciforte married Lucio Mastrogiovanni Tasca, the villa passed, together with the title of Conte di Almerita, to the family to whom it still belongs. This period saw the creation of the parterre in the irregularly shaped Romantic garden, with its exotic plants, the little lake with swans, the portico, and the little temple dedicated to Ceres, where, according to family tradition, Richard Wagner composed *Parsifal*. The Neoclassical structure of the building was not significantly altered by the works carried out in the Umbertan period. These include the plastering of the exterior and the decoration of the Neoclassical pediment with stucco figures supporting the arms of the Mastrogiovanni Tasca family.

Below and opposite
A *Rural Scene*, depicted in the central portion of the Neapolitan maiolica floor of one of the smaller rooms of the villa. The maiolica is dated and signed by its maker, Attanasio.

Palazzo Trigona di Canicarao in Noto

Noto is an outstanding example of all the towns that were completely rebuilt in southern Baroque style after the devastating earthquake of 1693. It is characterized, and rendered unique, by the golden colour of the fine-grained, delicate calcareous stone, particularly easy to cut, with which it was rebuilt on a gentle slope, at some distance from its original site. A stylistic unity was achieved by the combination of the building materials used by the architects and master craftsmen entrusted with the reconstruction of Noto, and the decision to make secular and religious buildings conform to a single model. This unity was acclaimed by the French Neoclassical architect Léon Dufourny, who worked in Palermo between 1789 and 1793. On a visit to Noto, he recorded his impressions: "The majority of these buildings and others of less importance seem to have been built in the same period, around 1702 ..., and by the same architect ... They are, at any rate, in the same style, and were designed by someone who has studied Palladio, Inigo Jones, and, above all, Vignola, and who has more or less copied their motifs." In

Above and opposite
The secondary façade and one of the two projecting wings roofed with a terrace on the side overlooking the garden.

addition, as an exponent of the current Neoclassicism, he noted: "The architecture is not always in the best taste, but at least the architectural orders, which are magnificent – particularly the Doric – are excellent and in some cases call to mind Vienna … The whole is very well-executed and produces a notable effect."

Indeed, according to Anthony Blunt, the architects involved in the reconstruction of the town, which continued throughout the eighteenth century, drew inspiration from the most disparate European models – from Austrian to French – known through engravings. The new layout of Noto conformed to modern criteria of regularity, having a grid-like structure consisting of three, main, parallel roads crossed at right angles by minor roads. Religious and secular buildings were lined up in an orderly fashion along the principal axes and around the three piazzas that open on to the main street. In the last third of the century, with the reconstruction of Palazzo Di Lorenzo and the building of the largest Baroque residences in the town by the important Astuto and Trigona families, the upper main road acquired prominence and became the favored area of the local aristocracy. The feud of Canicarao formed part of the territory of Modica, and belonged to the Cabrera family. After passing through various hands, it came into the possession of Paolo La Restia, who in 1627 was the first to be invested with the title of Marchese. It then passed through marriage to Tommaso Colonna Romano, Duca di Cesarò in 1634, and to the Trigona family in 1661, who are the current owners of the palace in Noto.

Its construction may be attributed to the patronage of Gaspare Maria Trigona – who was invested with the title of Canicarao in 1731 and eight years later with that of Marchese di Dainammare – or of his son, Bernardo Maria, who succeeded his father in 1777. It is one of the most

in a number of phases, all relatively close together. A plan of Noto made by Paolo Labisi around the middle of the eighteenth century shows that, at that time, the area where the palace was located had not yet been developed. The façade overlooking the street and the west wing were

Below and opposite
The Salone da Ballo (Ballroom) of the palace and the frieze that decorates the walls.

interesting examples of private building in the city, having the u-shaped structure typical of many of Noto's residential buildings, with the main façade on the street, a tower on each side and one in the center, and two projecting wings roofed with a terrace at the back. The façades, Baroque in decoration, are vertically divided by gigantic pilaster strips.

According to Stephen Tobriner, the palace was built

completed before the east wing, while the addition of the semicircular wall of the garden of the ground floor and the hanging garden to the east date from the nineteenth century. It has not as yet been possible to identify the architect responsible for the original design. One document refers to Bernardo Labisi, the son of the more famous Paolo, as the architect in charge of various works, though it also mentions an

"old cornice", which would suggest the existence of an earlier building. Indeed, a number of documentary sources record that, in 1770, Gaspare Maria Trigona had commissioned Paolo Labisi to design the new church of the monastery of S. Agata. The design pleased the Marchese, but the document states: "since the abovementioned gentleman was occupied with important business concerning his own house, he thought no more about it." About four years later, his son, Bernardo Maria, returned to the project, and, after a new design had been requested from the same architect, work on the new church finally began in 1755. Given the relationship between the Trigona family and Paolo Labisi during the 1770s – the very years in which the palace was built – it is possible that Labisi was also invited to design the new family residence. Entry to the palace is via the entrance on the main façade overlooking the street. A grand staircase then leads to the *piano nobile*. Here a series of rooms with ceilings decorated with grotesques constitutes a unique example of the palatial architecture of Noto. They have been attributed to Antonio Mazza and ascribed by Tobriner to the end of the 1770s (though perhaps dating from the early years of the nineteenth century).

Palazzo Beneventano del Bosco in Syracuse

According to Anthony Blunt, the palace of the Beneventano del Bosco family, which stands on the main piazza of Ortigia, the historic center of Syracuse, constitutes "one of the most perfect examples of Syracusan Baroque." It also marks an intense period of reconstruc- tion that began straight after the terrible earthquake of 1693 that devastated eastern Sicily. The oldest part of the building dates from the medieval period, when, as Privitera states, it belonged to the Arezzo della Targia and Borgia del Casale families. Throughout the seventeenth

century, the palace accommodated the Syracusan Order of St. John of Jerusalem, so-called because Syracuse was the last of the Order's Italian residences before its final move to Malta. In 1778, it was acquired by the Beneventano del Bosco family, to whom it still belongs.

The feud of Bosco di Schifano, or Alfano – as it is called in Francesco Sammartino De Spucches's *Storia dei feudi e dei titoli nobiliari di Sicilia* (A History of the Feuds and Noble Titles of Sicily) – was situated in the Val di Noto. The earliest surviving reference to it dates from 1296, when it belonged

Above
The courtyard of the palace, with its cobbled mosaic paving.

Right
The coat of arms of the Beneventano del Bosco family, surmounted by a triangular pediment, placed above the central balcony of the main façade.

to Simone Januensis da Lentini. After passing through various hands, in 1591 it was acquired by the Beneventano family. In the first half of the eighteenth century, the family seems to have enjoyed a period of considerable prosperity. Vincenzo Beneventano Ascenso, who was invested with Bosco di Schifano in 1729, acquired the feuds of Monteclimiti e Didini and of Casalgerardo Frescura e Belfronte. He was invested with the barony of these lands in 1734. Ten years later he also acquired the feud of Moriella. The refurbishment and modernization of the ancient medieval buildings of the palace in Syracuse may certainly be attributed to Vincenzo's son, Guglielmo Maria, who succeeded his father in 1752 and died in 1799.

Within the new structure of the Piazza del Duomo, which had been rebuilt – like much of the region – during the eighteenth century after the earthquake of 1693, Palazzo Beneventano was the most prominent seat of the aristocracy and of the balance that had been established between the aristocracy and temporal and ecclesiastical power. In turn, this was further represented by the Palazzo del Senato Cittadino (Palace of the Town Council), the Palazzo Vescovile (Bishop's Palace), and the cathedral. The cathedral was originally a Doric temple dating from the fifth century BC, later converted into a Christian church by the Normans. The

Norman façade was later replaced by a Baroque version, from the 1720s, designed by the architect Andrea Palma of Trapani.

In 1779 the Beneventano family entrusted the refurbishment of their house to the Syracusan architect Luciano Alì; this continued

until 1788. The work at the palace formed part of a profusion of architectural initiatives. These were promoted, from the 1770s onwards, by the city's rising noble and middle classes, in which Alì played a fundamental part, his masterpiece being Palazzo Beneventano. Having trained in Syracuse around the middle of the eighteenth century, in the circle of so-called craftsman-architects, Luciano Alì worked initially, in a subordinate position, on numerous religious buildings. Around 1760, he is mentioned in documents relating to the construction of a seminary under the direction of Alexandre Louis Demontier, a military engineer attached to the Bourbon court who was working in Syracuse. Demontier's French origins account for the elegant rocaille character of his works and the introduction of foreign models into the local architectural culture. The encounter with Demontier must have been crucial for Alì, whose personality has recently been reappraised in the context of eighteenth-century Sicilian archiecture.

At Palazzo Beneventano, Alì, now a mature artist, and having attained recognition as an architect in that very period, embarked on a series of works on the medieval part of the building. He altered the façade, raising the attic and adding the balconies and the great convex entrance. Using a design which was unprecedented in Sicily but inspired by treatises and by certain

Below and opposite
A spiral staircase from the medieval period still exists inside the palace.

contemporary Neapolitan constructions, he built the grand staircase *ex novo*, described by Anthony Blunt as "without a doubt, one of the most elegant external staircases in the whole of Sicily." It served as a partition in the double courtyard, before the arches, which were originally open, were walled up or glassed in. In the same period he made alterations to the interior, removing old structures that were incompatible with the new layout. Ermenegildo Martorana from Palermo produced frescoes and sopraporta oil-paintings for the rooms of the *piano nobile*, while the ceilings of the other apartments were decorated with paintings using Neoclassical themes.

Palazzo Beneventano del Bosco became the most impressive house in the city. In keeping with its reputation, it was selected in 1806 as the most suitable venue for the fashionable reception arranged in honour of Ferdinand IV, who made a brief visit to the city during the second residence of the Bourbon court in Sicily.

Below and opposite
The hall of the palace, its ceiling decorated by Ermenegildo Martorana.

Villa Ajroldi in Palermo

At the end of the eight-eenth century, Colli plain, a holiday location favored by the Palermitan aristocracy, second only to Bagheria in popularity, wit-nessed a considerable amount of new construction. In one of the districts closest to the city, at the foot of Monte Pellegrino, stands Villa Ajroldi, at one time sur-rounded by extensive grounds which were later incorpo-rated into the park of La Favorita. In its earliest days the villa belonged to Girolamo Riggio, Marchese di Ginestra, who built the first wing around the middle of the eighteenth century. The construction was con-tinued by Stefano Ajroldi, President of the High Court, and "perfected" by his brother, Monsignor Alfonso Ajroldi, Judge of the Royal Monarchy, and Chief Chaplain.

The villa must have enjoyed considerable prestige even at the time of its con-struction. Gaspare Palermo, scholar and near-contemporary commentator, the author of a guide to the city published in 1816, described it as one "of the most magnificent, to rival any other in Italy or else-where. Outside, the house

presents a well-designed and handsome façade, with busts of Carrara marble, and is enclosed by a long fence of iron railings, broken up by pillars supporting numerous busts of white marble."

A watercolor from the end of the nineteenth century shows the villa prior to its extended for several hectares opposite the main façade.

It is not known when the villa was constructed, nor which architect was responsible for the design, but its characteristics correspond to the Neoclassical culture of the second half of the eighteenth century. The plan,

being engulfed by the city and before the railings outside the main façade were moved back. At that time it was surrounded by a "number of gardens, containing broad, spacious paths and long avenues, shaded by tall, leafy trees, many of them exotic, and finally large cultivated fields" (Gaspare Palermo). Statues and fountains were placed in the vast park that sober and severe, consists of a principal block, rectangular in form, to which two wings, consisting of servants' quarters, have been added, both originally roofed with a terrace, forming a horseshoe-shaped courtyard. The main façade is divided horizontally by simple fascias and vertically by pilaster strips, single or double, which form lighter elements against the darker

Below
The Banquet of the Gods painted
on the ceiling of the reception
room is inspired by Raphael's
painting for the Villa Farnesina
in Rome.

Below
The Banquet of the Gods painted
on the ceiling of the reception
room is inspired by Raphael's
painting for the Villa Farnesina
in Rome.

background of the plaster which, on the *piano nobile*, frame eleven windows with alternating triangular and curved tympanums. The centrally situated entrance is flanked by columns with Corinthian capitals and Attic bases. On the *piano nobile* there is a balcony which is larger than those on either side of it. A balustrade decorated with marble busts and a central escutcheon carved with the coat of arms of the Ajroldi family, runs around the top of the building.

On the façade overlooking the garden, an interesting design was used for the central section, consisting of a rustic base and a huge triangular tympanum at the top. This part of the villa, flanked by two porticos on the ground floor covered with terraces at second-floor level, contains the great, red marble staircase, erected inside the building, as was the custom in the villas of Palermo and Bagheria in the late eighteenth century. The staircase has a pincer-like form, in which the two arms open out to give independent access to each of the two wings of the *piano nobile*.

The decoration of the ceiling of the principal room of the villa, located in the left wing of the second floor, belongs to the same sober, classicizing cultural climate as the exterior. It is signed by Giuseppe Crestadoro and dated 1781. As often happened in the Neoclassical period, when Raphael was most popular, Crestadoro

used engravings made from the painted decoration of the Farnesina in Rome when executing his own frescoes. The *Council of the Gods* and the *Presentation of Psyche to Jove* are exact reproductions. The right wing is the more interesting part of the villa. It contains a series of moderately sized

Opposite
The entrance to the private apartments of the right wing of the villa.

Below
The Salotto Rosso (Red Room), situated in the right wing of the villa, is decorated with stucco both on the walls and on the ceiling.

rooms; some may have been created out of a larger reception room, balancing the one in the left wing. The style of the decoration suggests that these rooms may date from a slightly earlier period than the fully Neoclassical room painted by Crestadoro. The ceilings are elegantly decorated with delicate rocaille stuccowork. This runs across the vault in curvilinear patterns and vegetal and floral motifs, enclosing small landscapes and still-lifes, depicting pergolas, and framing open skies crossed by painted birds of all kinds. In some rooms the stuccowork continues down onto the walls, creating false sopraporta panels depicting plants and birds. In the Salotto Rosso (Red Room), situated next to the entrance, thin stucco pilaster strips decorated with a buttercup motif divide up the surface of the walls, reproducing on a smaller scale an idea used in the great Salone da Ballo (Ballroom) of Palazzo Ajutamicristo. In the Galleria the stucco decoration of the ceiling continues to the doors and mirrors, following a unitary stylistic design. Tall, painted fascias cover the lower part of the walls, reaching down to the glazed maiolica floor with its geometric pattern. Several rooms are characterized by a touch of chinoiserie, where the wooden paneling of the walls is linked to the ceiling by stucco corner-strips. Landscapes are depicted in relief on the strips and the console tables beneath them must once have held oriental porcelain.

The apartments of the right wing were probably the fruits of an extremely refined taste, according to Gaspare Palermo, meriting "detailed observation on account of the magnificence of the halls and rooms, arranged and decorated with the most refined taste, with frescoes on the ceiling,

canvases of great artistry, and delicate and polished works of gilded carving."

Below and opposite
The distinctive features of the Galleria, situated in the right wing of the villa, are the stucco corner-strips with Chinese-style depictions and the console tables for oriental porcelain.

Below
The ceiling of the Galleria is decorated with stucco floral and vegetal motifs and painted birds.

Opposite
One of the above-door panels, consisting of an oil-on-canvas *Still Life*.

Following pages
The ceiling of one of the rooms in the right wing, and, to the right, a detail of the decoration using stucco and paint.

Villa Spedalotto at Bagheria

The custom of *villeggiatura* – taking a holiday in the country – spread rapidly among the wealthier members of the aristocracy. In the course of the eighteenth century, the number of villas at Bagheria rose from the twenty or so that existed at the beginning of the century to more than three times that number. With the improvement of the main roads, it became easier to move about, with the result that periods spent in the country became longer. The construction of new villas on the lower part of the Piana di Bagheria – Villa Cattolica, first and foremost, Villa Aragona (later Villa Cutò), Villa Rammacca, and Villa Sant'Isidoro – led to the increased importance of a stretch of road, probably dating from the seventeenth century, that diverted the course of the consular road, the ancient Via Valeria that ran from Marsala to Messina, taking it closer to the coast. Thus, the villa of the Branciforte family, situated in the interior of the plain and now surrounded by a sizeable collection of houses, found itself isolated.

It was in response to this situation that the shape of Bagheria changed during the

Above
The secondary façade of the villa, overlooking a citrus plantation.

Opposite
The projecting pronaos of the principal façade.

second half of the eighteenth century. Between 1768 and 1772, Salvatore Branciforte, Principe di Butera, commissioned the architects Paolo Vivaldi and Salvatore Attinelli to create a new road. It was to be broad and straight and connect the two parts of Bagheria; the lower part, which had developed around the villas on the consular road, and the upper part around Villa Butera. Standing at the end of the new road – named Corso Butera – its position raised and with a new orientation, the villa of the Branciforte family once again dominated the plain below.

At the point where Corso Butera crossed the consular road, a large, irregularly shaped piazza was created, called Punta Aguglia. Here the Principi di Cattolica and the Naselli d'Aragona family erected stone rotundas and monumental arches in front of their villas, thereby challenging the revived supremacy of the Butera family and affirming the greatness of their own noble houses. The classicist taste of the late eighteenth century that so despised the bizarre Baroque character of the villas at Bagheria delighted in the simplicity and regularity of the new style of urban planning favoured by the Principe di Butera. The Neoclassical architect Léon Dufourny, active in Palermo between 1789 and 1793, noted the accuracy and pleasant appearance of the architecture of the houses overlooking the Corso Butera. The German Jacques

Ignaz Hittorff, one of the chief figures in the urban renovation of Paris in the nineteenth century, during a visit to Sicily in 1823 considered Villa Aragona to be the only house in Bagheria worthy of being immortalized by his pen. The young Karl Friedrich Schinkel, destined

Below
The little chapel in one of the reception rooms.

Opposite
The terrace overlooking the citrus plantation, which stretches down to the sea.

to become one of the most important German architects of the nineteenth century, was in Italy between 1803 and 1805.

Like Goethe, Schinkel regarded his stay in Sicily as a crucial stage in his journey.

He was deeply impressed by the intimate relationship between the landscape, of extraordinary beauty, and the architecture, both classical and Neoclassical. When he arrived at Bagheria, it was the surrounding countryside, rather than the buildings, that drew his attention. Apart from Villa Butera, the only house in the area to appear among his sketches is Villa Paternò di Spedalotto. Its position – it was once immersed in greenery – and its architectural character

partly corresponded to the taste and the culture of late eighteenth-century Germany, which wavered between the Neoclassical and the pre-Romantic. Documentary sources indicate that the villa was commissioned by Don Barbaro Arezzo in 1783 from the architect Emmanuele Cardona (or Incardona), a member of a family of wood engravers and a pupil of Giuseppe Venanzio Marvuglia, the chief exponent of Sicilian Neoclassicism.

Above and right
The Galleria overlooking the terrace. Mythological scenes are painted on the walls.

According to the records, the still-unfinished villa was bought by the Paternò family, Baroni and later Marchesi of Spedalotto, to whom it still belongs. The family had acquired the title as a result of the marriage, in 1784, of Onofrio Emanuele Paternò, the younger son of the Barone di Raddusa, and Maria Antonia Trigona, Baronessa di Cugno e Spedalotto, the last member of her family. Their son, Vincenzo, married Maria Concetta Ventimiglia e Moncada, thereby acquiring for his heirs the titles of Conte di Prades, Marchese di Regiovanni, and Barone di Pettineo.

As was customary for Sicilian country houses, Villa Spedalotto was encircled by a line of low buildings which accommodated the servants. The owners of the building have traditionally maintained that an original plan provided for a two-storey building, which was then realized only in part. In fact, because the house was built on a terraced slope, the principal floor is level with the ground only on the main façade, while on the façade overlooking the sea it forms the second floor, lying above what may at one time have been the guest quarters. This lower floor has barrel-vaulted ceilings and fine maiolica floors contemporary with the building.

The Neoclassical main façade of the villa, which is on one level only, is characterized by a projecting pronaos, hexastyle, of the Doric order, which, being the only novel

Right
The barrel-vaulted ceiling of the Galleria, decorated with Neoclassical motifs.

element within an eighteenth-century structure, has been judged by Gioacchino Lanza Tomasi to be an addition from the end of the century. Paintings depicting mythological scenes, surrounded by frames consisting of classical motifs and flanked by allegorical figures such as the *Four Seasons* and the *Four Continents*, decorate the walls and ceiling of the principal room. Arranged in a line, one after the other, again in accordance with the canons of the eighteenth century, the reception rooms open onto a handsome terrace overlooking a citrus plantation that extends to the sea. The decoration of the dining room and the private apartments is lighter and more lively, with grotesques, playing putti, and small animals.

Indicated by the Marchese di Villabianca as one of the twenty-two finest villas in Bagheria, Villa Spedalotto has had a number of distinguished guests. During the first period when the Bourbon court was resident in Sicily, between 1798 and 1802, Ferdinand IV and Maria Carolina stayed at Villa Valguarnera while the heirs apparent – the future king of Naples, Francis I, and his wife, Maria Clementina – stayed at Villa Spedalotto, as a plaque above the entrance records. In 1810 the house witnessed the birth of the so-called "Re Bomba", Ferdinand of the Two Sicilies, the son of Francesco, first Duca di Calabria and Vicar of the Kingdom of Sicily from 1812. Finally, it welcomed Louis-Philippe d'Orleans and, at the end of the nineteenth century, the great Jesuit mathematician and astronomer, Angelo Secchi, whose marble bust stands at the entrance to the villa.

Palazzina Cinese in Palermo

In his *Diario di un giacobino* published in 1790, the architect Léon Dufourny, then living in Palermo, left an account of an inspection of the then still-unfinished house of Benedetto Lombardo e Lucchesi, a judge of the great civil and criminal court of the realm. He went there with his colleague Giuseppe Venanzio Marvuglia – a renowned exponent of the Neoclassical in Sicily – who had drawn the plans and was directing the work, though the client's part in the venture was central. "Il construit là pour cet avocat un casin soit disant chinois mais outre que ce caractère y est totalment manqué, la décoration et distribution en sont mauvaisee et sans style …" ["For that lawyer he built a house there, ostensibly in the Chinese manner, except that the Chinese character is totally lacking, the decoration and the proportions are poor and without style."] This observation was made by Dufourny, an absolute purist of Neoclassicism, adding to his comments with a sketch of the building in the margin. This shows the first arrangement "in the Chinese manner" of the structure, which subsequently underwent various stages of modification.

Above
The Palazzina Cinese: watercolor (1790–1797), by Pietro Martorana, now in the Palazzo Reale in Palermo.

Opposite
The main façade of the Palazzina Cinese.

A second building phase is documented in a watercolor by Pietro Martorana in the collections of the Palazzo Reale in Palermo; it was painted before 1797, the year in which the artist died. It shows galleries with wooden railings that surround the building at two levels and pagoda roofs. The Marchese di Villabianca notes in his diary that he had visited the palazzina, which was "entirely built on a wooden framework; the balconies, consisting of planks supported by structures of wood and rope, go round the house and are in the Chinese fashion and taste; there are little bells dangling, which ring when the wind blows, and that is why it is known as the villa of the bells". He adds: "To me, Villabianca, who visited it in May of 1798, it seemed an eccentric building that would not endure, completely lacking in grandeur."

During the eighteenth century, examples of chinoiserie spread throughout Europe, where the fascination with all things oriental had been stimulated by the publication of accounts of voyages and of tracts on China. France was the custodian of a significant example of chinoiserie in the *Trianon de porcelaine* at Versailles, and there were examples in Russia and in other parts of Italy.

A magnificent porcelain-room was built between 1757 and 1759 in the Palazzo Reale di Portici, near Naples, commissioned by the Bourbons. In Sicily, from the middle of

the century, every self-respecting palazzo contained at least one room decorated in the Chinese manner: for example, the extraordinary Palazzo Valguarnera-Gangi in Palermo and the Palazzo Biscari in Catania. But, as far as is known, the Palazzina Cinese is the first example of

chinoiserie in Sicily to involve the building of an entire house, an event that no doubt set off the unfavorable criticism of contemporaries. New prospects for the Lombardo family and new phases of restructuring of the Palazzina Cinese were being anticipated on the eve of the arrival, in December 1798, of Ferdinand and Maria Carolina of Bourbon in flight from Naples. Escorted by the English fleet commanded by

Admiral Nelson, they arrived in Palermo, where they established their residence. The aristocracy of Palermo vied to receive them when it was revealed His Royal Majesty was looking for several places in the country which would serve for his delight. Numerous landowners such as the owners of the casina di Lombardo, the Principe di Malvagna, the Marchese Vannucci, the Principe di Niscemi, the son of the Duca di Pietratagliata, and the Marchese Don Stefano Ajroldi, all with properties in the plain of Colli, freely offered parcels of land ... The king did not accept the gift, but wishing to have the pleasure of the acquisition, paid the rent, ... "his royal heart remaining greatly pleased with the kind affection and attention of the owners to his royal person".

Among the generous notables intent on securing a place in the good graces of the king was Giuseppe Maria Lombardo e Lucchese, Barone delle Scale e di Manchi di Belice, who had in the previous year inherited the property in the Colli plain from his brother Benedetto. At the request of Benedetto's creditors, the palazzina had been put up for sale on a long lease. Marvuglia, called in to evaluate the work completed and still to be done on the construction to set the annual rent, has left an accurate description. Together with the watercolor by Martorana and an album of drawings by Alessandro Emmanuele

Marvuglia for the execution of the new and definitive plans for the house and its surroundings, the 1799 description makes it possible to reconstruct the state of the building in minute detail at the time when the Bourbons acquired it. The reception rooms were located at the centre of the building (the billiard room in the basement and the *salone* on the *piano nobile*), while the private apartments were at the sides of the palazzina. The pictorial decoration had already been planned and the artists who were to carry it out had already been engaged – they were artists who also worked under Ferdinando, like the painter Benedetto Cotardi, a Neapolitan active in Sicily for the past thirty years assisting Andrea Gigante and Marvuglia.

While these arrangements were taking place, the royal family settled in, and initially, from 1799 to 1800, work started on the park and on the wall that surrounded it; documents attest to the presence, in those same years, of Elia Interguglielmi, responsible for the pictorial decorations of the king's bedroom, and of Benedetto Cotardi, responsible for completing existing work and painting variations on existing themes.

The park was embellished with statues, fountains and ornaments, and equipped with a number of service buildings and structures in eclectic taste – aqueducts, cellars, storerooms, stables. In the Italian garden behind the house, the marble worker

Giosué Durante made several white marble basins with artificial grottoes "in the Chinese manner" (1800). A *cafeaos* (Sicilian transliteration of "coffeehouse") was also set up there, and, on the right-hand side as one entered, the "barracks of the cavalry of the royal huntsmen". Giuseppe Patricolo, royal master builder, built two spiral staircases at the sides of the house. A "mathematical table that rises and descends", made to a design that came from Naples and similar to the one that Louis XV had installed at the petit Trianon at Versailles, was placed in the dining room; it follows from Dufourny's notes that the table had been included in the original scheme.

With the collapse of the Neapolitan republic and the subsequent restoration, the royal court returned to Naples from 1802 to 1805, but with the return of the French, it had to take refuge in Palermo for the second time. It may have been the absence of the court that made a comprehensive reconstruction of the house possible: the reconstruction was completed by 1807, judging by the *Inventario generale del Real Casino della Real Villa dei Colli, denominata "La Favorita"*, published in that year. At the same time, conspicuous sums continued to be provided for the hunting lodge near the forest of Ficuzza. It follows from the 1807 inventory that a large part of the furnishings had come from the royal site of

San Leucio, the Palazzo Reale at Portici, and the Villa Favorita in Naples. Despite the fact that the critics are agreed in attributing the plans for the reconstruction to Giuseppe Venanzio, the documents name Alessandro Emmanuele Marvuglia as director of works from 1802;

it was he who, from 1804, saw to the new "restoration" of the house. The pagoda roofs at either side of the taller, central portion of the house were removed and replaced by terraces. Two polygonal porticoes were added at the centers of the main façades and the interiors were modified. In 1803 to 1804, the Neoclassical chapel was added to the right of the

Left and opposite
The dining room and adjoining room, both with walls and ceilings completely covered with paintings of oriental scenes of country life.

main façade: its dome was supported on eight columns with Ionic capitals, and arcades ran along its walls. The eclectic decorations of the private apartments and the reception rooms, in taste that varies from the Chinese to the Turkish and from the Pompeian to the Neoclassical, were finished later, during the second sojourn of the king, from 1805 to 1815. After the rebuilding was completed, the most important rooms were decorated by Rosario Silvestri and Benedetto Cotardi, employed to paint decorative motifs, and Vincenzo Riolo and Giuseppe Velasco, who did the figurative painting; these two were later involved in work at the Palazzo Reale, yet again in the employ of the Bourbons.

The Palazzina Cinese thus assumed its present aspect: a rectangular building on four floors, of which one is a basement, partly below ground level; a portico, the width of the central part of the building, projects forwards beyond the main elevation. The outside of the palazzina is red and ochre in color. In addition to the two external spiral staircases mentioned above, which afford access to the third floor, a double staircase leads to the portico on the southern elevation, and, through this, to the raised *piano nobile*. Under the double staircase, a door leads into the basement, and to the ballroom which occupies nearly all of it. The ceiling of the ballroom is decorated with architectural ruins in *trompe*

l'oeil, and scenes and figures in the Neoclassical style are painted in the panels on the walls; these decorations are attributed to Raimondo Gioia. A series of galleries connect the basement with the adjacent pavilions.

The rooms in the central area of the *piano nobile* have silk wall hangings painted in vegetable dyes, apparently by Vincenzo Riolo. In the *salone* – where receptions and audiences were held – the ceiling, painted with oriental scenes has been attributed to Rosario Silvestri and Vincenzo Riolo. These two also worked together in the Herculaneum room, where Silvestri painted the ceiling and Riolo was responsible for the twelve oil paintings of women on the walls. The dining room, in which the table with the mechanical contrivance is still preserved, is also on this floor. Decorated with small columns, the walls and ceiling of this room are painted with scenes of oriental country life. On the western side of the *piano nobile* are the royal apartments, containing the bedroom with a baldacchino and columns, the painted ceiling of which is attributed to Giuseppe Velasco and Benedetto Cotardi. On this ceiling, a false arcade with pointed arches is depicted, with people in oriental dress leaning on the balustrades.

Maria Carolina's apartments are on the third floor. The decoration of the bedroom – attributed to Benedetto Cotardi – is Neoclassical in style, with

Below and opposite
Details of the ceiling of the *salone* in the center of the *piano nobile*, used for receptions and audiences. The frescoes with oriental scenes are attributed to Rosario Silvestri and Vincenzo Riolo.

pavilions, moldings and decorative motifs. A room in the central part of the third floor, flanked by the two terraces, was furnished in the Turkish fashion, with columns. Above this is the "stanza dei venti", also known as the "specola" or observatory, with an octagonal ceiling and decoration

Palermo, which installed the Museo Etnografico Siciliano Pitré and the Giuseppe Pitré Library of Folklore in two of the buildings in the park.

Below and opposite
Oriental figures painted on the walls of the drawing room.

attributed to Rosario Silvestri and his colleagues. After the annexation of Sicily by Italy, the Palazzina Cinese was included among the real estate assigned to the Italian crown, and in 1877 it passed on to the state. In 1935, the palazzina in the Parco della Favorita was let to the city of

Castello di Donnafugata in Ragusa

Around the second half of the nineteenth century, Corrado Arezzo e de Spuches, Barone di Donnafugata, had a sumptuous residence built a few kilometers from Ragusa. It was in an enormous park that had formerly contained abundant hot springs and he built it around an extant core. Born in 1824, he had studied with the Oratorians in Palermo, which was, at that time, in the throes of major urban development. Corrado received his training during the period when the revival of earlier styles of art, eclecticism, and the passion for botany and agriculture were all fashionable. This cultural climate, while it encouraged the revival of the Greek or medieval traditions of Sicily, by the same token undermined the political movement that campaigned for autonomy. An art collector, poet and music lover, Corrado was also an industrialist and a politician. He had been involved in the revolution and was elected, to add to his other responsibilities, to the Sicilian parliament in 1848.

Like many other Sicilian placenames, Donnafugata is of Arabic origin. The prefix "donna" appears often in a series of other names, and

Above
View of the western façade of the Castello di Donnafugata.

Opposite
The neo-Gothic arcade in the southern façade, designed at the end of the nineteenth century by Saverio Castillet.

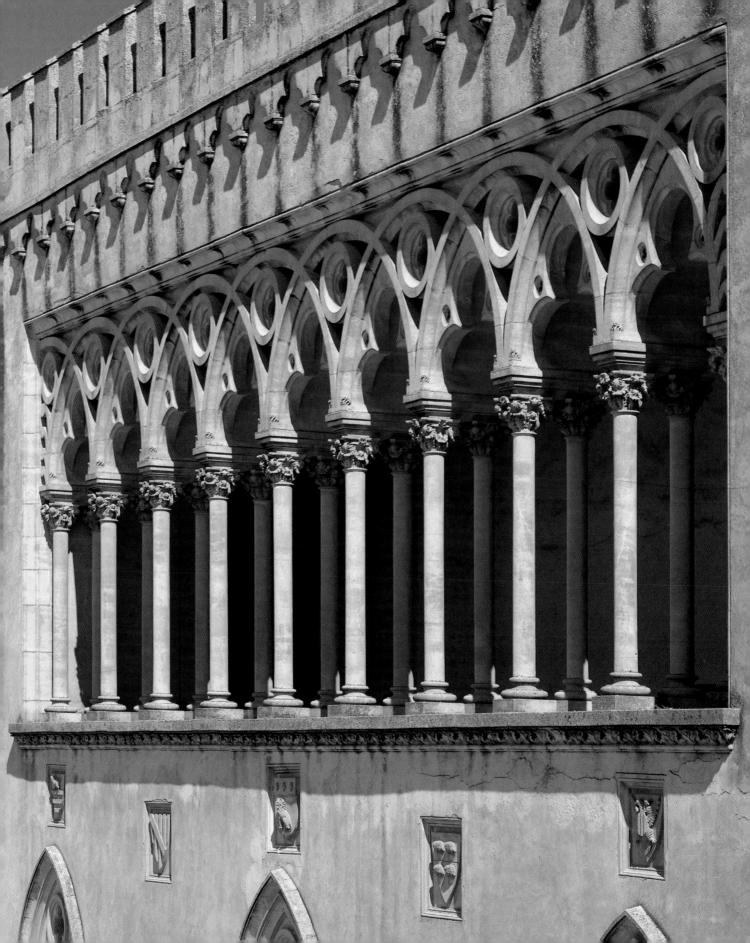

derives from the Arabic *ain*. In the *Dizionario topografico della Sicilia*, published in 1855, Vito Amico makes reference to Donnalucata – *Aynlucata* in Latin – which is also in the province of Ragusa. He states that "Ayn in the Saracen language" means "spring". Donnafugata, which does not appear in the dictionary, would derive from *ain as iafaiat*, which means "spring of health". Even though this may be the correct etymology, an assortment of legends has grown up around the name Donnafugata with the principal one concerning Blanche of Navarre, regent of Sicily. It is said that in 1412, the queen, pursued by Conte Bernardo di Cabrera, Chief Justice of the Realm and pretender to the throne, was imprisoned by him in the castello.

In fact, the domain of Donnafugata belonged to the Cabrera family until the middle of the seventeenth century. In 1648, it was awarded to Vincenzo Arezzo La Rocca, Barone di Serri. There is very little information about the original seventeenth-century core of the castello. Scholars have traced a few pictures of the building, which show the stages in the transformation from the original *baglio* to the castello inspired by examples of the neo-Gothic. In the earliest of these representations, a detail of the wall paintings in the music room within the castello, a few elements of the present circuit of walls – such as the angular turrets that were the

Below
A carved corbel of one of the external windows.

Opposite
View from within the neo-Gothic arcade in the southern façade.

inspiration for Renaissance examples – are already visible. The crenelated wall is the result of an initial renovation, designed to surround the original irregularly shaped structure with a rectangular enclosure. Next, a new, vaguely Neoclassical building was added, as shown

Below and opposite
Airy structures such as the "coffeehouse" and the small circular neoclassical temple are to be found in the beautiful garden.

in a watercolor in the collections of the castello. In an anonymous painting, also in the collection, the home of the Arezzo family had already assumed its neo-Gothic appearance, except for a few discrepancies in the doors and windows – one of the three mullioned windows, for example, is no longer there. Lastly, the square northwest tower in the Gothic style was added for reasons of symmetry after 1906, the year to which another watercolor showing the castello can be dated.

The fortified medieval appearance of the northern and eastern sides of the castello is in contrast to that of its other faces. The southern façade was broken through at the end of the nineteenth century to make a long arcade – the work of Saverio Castillet – described as "faithful copy ... of the arcade of the Palazzo dei Papi (Palace of the Popes) at Viterbo". On the western face, the enclosing wall consists of a row of low buildings surmounted by terraces with an open view of the landscape.

An avenue, flanked by a row of low service buildings, leads to the forecourt in front of the southern side of the castello, which is surrounded by an immense park established by Corrado. On the right as one enters the park, a stairway leads from the lodge into the garden, and, via a long straight avenue to the "coffeehouse". To the right of this avenue there was once a

small botanical garden, about which Corrado was passionate. To the left was a superb garden with a labyrinth, grottoes, fountains, curious statues, and *jeux d'eau*, conceived in the sixteenth-century Tuscan-Roman manner. Some examples of such gardens must already have existed in Sicily – the garden villa of Ercole Branciforte at Cammarata was a well-known instance. The Park at Donnafugata also has a small round temple, a recurring theme in Palermo in the Neoclassical period – the example in the Villa Belmonte all'Acquasanta epitomizes them – and a little mock church where, if you place your foot on the second of the steps leading up to it, the door suddenly opens and an automaton in the habit of a friar welcomes you with an embrace. Opposite the northern façade is the double *parterre*, or formal flower garden à la française; beyond that a cypress grove surrounds two Neoclassical cenotaphs.

The portal to the castello is on the southern front. A passage leads to a square courtyard, from which a second, smaller passage leads on to the grand staircase adorned with statues that leads to the *piano nobile*. Here a series of rooms, with a large part of their original furnishings still preserved, lead into one another. The first – called the salone degli stemmi because the walls are decorated with the armorial bearings of a very large number of noble Sicilian families – leads on one side to the wing with

Right
The sumptuous hall of mirrors.

the hall of mirrors and to the billiard room. On the other side are the rooms in the seventeenth-century core of the building, of which the music room is outstanding. Here, between the ceiling and the lower parts of the walls, which are decorated with classical motifs, a false arcade with columns opens on a more or less imaginary view. The prospect is a seventeenth-century caprice, in which buildings that really existed – the pavilion of the Botanical Garden, a fundamental achievement of Palermo Neoclassicism, and the original Villa di Donnafugata – alternate with arcadian landscapes and classical buildings scattered here and there.

In 1878 Corrado's granddaughter married the Vicomte Gaetano Combes de Lestrade. The couple had several rooms in the northwestern part of the castello redecorated in the French style; among these was the blue bedroom, situated in the tower and therefore circular.

The name Donnafugata is now very well-known, thanks to *Il Gattopardo* (The Leopard), by Giuseppe Tomasi di Lampedusa. Except for its name, the fictional home of the Principe di Salina bears no resemblance to Donnafugata. That should rather be identified with the country seat of Lampedusa's mother, the palazzo of the Filangeri family, Principi di Cutò, at Santa Margherita Belice in western Sicily.

Below
One of the drawing rooms of the Castello di Donnafugata.

Opposite
The pavilion of the botanical gardens in Palermo, as seen in a wall painting in the music room. A false arcade opens on views of landscapes and buildings.

Villa Whitaker in Palermo

A fundamental chapter in the political, economic and social history of nineteenth-century Sicily is marked by the presence of a colony of affluent middle-class English entrepreneurs, who were both intelligent and intellectual.

Although the great influx of English families arrived on the island during the first few years of the nineteenth century, the Woodhouses had disembarked at Marsala as early as 1773 and had started a flourishing wine business, producing in addition to exporting. John Woodhouse, who had acquired an old tunny fishery with a Palladian villa, was a great friend of Nelson's, to whom Ferdinand of Bourbon, King of the Two Sicilies, had given the duchy of Bronte on the slopes of Mount Etna. Because of the Napoleonic blockade, English merchants on the continent were forced to find new bases in the Mediterranean. Thus, between 1806 and 1813, when Sicily to all intents and purposes became a British colony, the Woodhouse monopoly was undermined. The English installed themselves mainly around Trapani and Messina, widened their activities to include banking

Above
The main façade of the Villa Whitaker.

Opposite
The entrance in the main façade of the villa.

and trade in a great variety of products – in addition, of course, to fortified wines, and particularly marsala. Of the commercial empires built up in Sicily by the Hopps, Wood, and Corlett families, to name but a few, that of the Ingham-Whitakers, small landowners from Yorkshire, was in the

Marsala and Castelvetrano, he preferred to settle in Palermo, first in a house in the plain of Sant'Oliva, then in the Palazzo Ingham, which he built – it is now the Grand Hotel et des Palmes in Via Roma. In the middle of the 1820s, Benjamin was already the richest of the foreign

Below
The park contains an abundance of venerable exotic plants.

Opposite
The colonnaded entrance in the main façade.

vanguard. In 1806, Benjamin Ingham, the founder of the enterprise, came to Sicily as a very young man. Although he owned a string of *bagli* (warehouses for wine) between

merchants in Sicily and had entered the cream of Palermo society: he married Alessandra Spadafora, Duchessa di Santa Rosalia, and was awarded the title of Barone di Manchi e

Following pages
The cast iron and glass orangery on one side of the villa, designed by Ignazio Greco and made by the Izzambert foundry in Paris, exterior and interior views.

Scala. Benjamin asked his nephew, Joseph Whitaker – a talented businessman – to join him. Joseph married Sophia Sanderson, daughter of the British consul at Messina; in honor of the marriage, he built the Villa Sophia in the Colli area – then still open country – near Palermo. With the aid of Joseph, the family business became the largest wine enterprise in Marsala.

Of Joseph and Sophia's twelve children, only three remained in Sicily: Joshua, known as Joss, Robert, called Bob, and Joseph Isaac or Pip. Now entirely accepted by Palermo society of the *belle époque*, the young scions of the family fostered the worldly as well as the intellectual life of the city, and surrounded themselves with eminent representatives of the oldest aristocratic Sicilian families, the entrepreneurial upper-middle classes, politicians and intellectuals, especially foreigners. They built new houses and embellished those already in the family: Bob and his wife Maude Bennet moved into the Villa Sophia, while Joss and his wife Euphrosyne Manuel, the owner of a renowned and very rich collection of Trapani corals, lived in the Villa Whitaker, now the prefecture, which they built in the Venetian Gothic style.

In 1883, Pip married Tina Scalia, a leading figure in English society in Palermo at the end of the century and daughter of the famous general who distinguished himself at the time of Garibaldi's exploits.

Extremely talented in both commerce and business, Pip was an eclectic spirit. It is he who identified the island of San Pantaleo, just off the coast north of Marsala, as the Punic island of Mozia, and began a long campaign of excavations which are still in progress. He was an expert ornithologist

Below
The dining room.

Opposite
The wooden ceiling of the dining room.

who assembled a valuable collection of stuffed birds, later sold to a museum in Belfast, and published *Birds of Tunisia*, a work in two volumes. As a result of many voyages to America and the tropics, he was also an authority on botany and established one of the most luxuriant, spectacular and innovative parks in all of Sicily around his villa. Between 1885 and 1886, Pip and Tina acquired a property of about ten hectares in Malfitano, an area then isolated and far from the historic center of Palermo, which was suffering a long period of neglect and decline just at that time. Malfitano was one of the areas of new urban development along the axis of the Via Ruggero Settimo and the Strada della Libertà in the late nineteenth century.

The plans for the villa were entrusted to Ignazio Greco, who was asked to emulate the Villa Favard on the Lungarno Vespucci in Florence, which had been designed by Giuseppe Poggi in 1857. Although the terms of the contract allowed little freedom, the directives of the client matched the talents of the architect, who united knowledge of recent technological advances – probably acquired during a stay in Paris – with a taste for the Neoclassic, clearly identifiable on the exterior in the recapitulation of sixteenth-century conventions. The wrought and cast-iron components, ordered from a foundry in Paris, comprise the most original parts of the building: the orangery, the verandas, and the stairs.

The interior of the villa is arranged in the classical eighteenth-century manner, with the raised *piano nobile* used for reception rooms and the upper story for the private apartments.

Each room, however, had taken on a character of its own: there were no rows of

nearly identical *saloni*, but secluded rooms that reflected the modern need for privacy, intimacy and functionality. There are Louis XV and Louis XVI drawing rooms, a billiard room, a dining room, a smoking room, a library, a ballroom and the so-called summer room. A grandiose corridor richly decorated with pictures in the Pompeian style, as well as nineteenth-

Below
The summer room with walls painted by Ettore De Maria Bergler.

Opposite
A corner of the smoking room.

century Sicilian paintings, and *objets d'art* – outstanding among these are two cloisonnés elephants from the imperial palace in Beijing and the Gobelin tapestries on the walls of the grand staircase – connected the other rooms, but had the additional purpose of emphasizing the prominent social position of the Whitaker family. The ceiling of the corridor-gallery, divided into bays by barrel and cross vaults, was decorated in Pompeian style in the fashion of the time, which combined floral motifs and grotesque figures with a taste for chinoiserie and archaeology, while a few arcadian scenes and mythological landscapes were placed at the centres of the vaults; the staircase which led to the upper story in an exceedingly elegant curve was similarly decorated.

The work was entrusted to Rocco Lentini (a painter from Palermo and a pupil of Francesco Lo Jacono), under whose direction worked the most fashionable artists of the time: besides the stucco worker Enea and the wood carver Salvatore Valenti, Giovanni Nicolini was responsible for the pictures in the corridor; Ettore De Maria Bergler painted a most authentic-looking artificial garden, full of exotic plants and populated with various species of birds in the summer room, and, together with Francesco Padovano, decorated the two drawing rooms. Villa Whitaker is a splendid and characteristic

Below
Upper part of the stairwell, with three Gobelin tapestries depicting stories from the Aeneid.

Opposite
The staircase leading to the private apartments, embellished with statues and tapestries.

Above and opposite
A shipwreck woven into one of the Gobelin tapestries depicting stories from the Aeneid in the music room.

expression of its times, although it does contain, in embryonic form, some elements of the grand Art Nouveau period of Palermo. Shortly after this, Lentini and De Maria Bergler worked together again, this time on the decorations of the Teatro Massimo under Ernesto Basile. He was deemed the greatest architect of that most distinctive cultural fusion, of which Palermo was one of the main centers.

Villa Bordonaro alle Croci in Palermo

Palermo was, for the most part, confined within seventeenth-century city walls until the early years of the nineteenth century, when a program of urban expansion began, which gave rise to the configuration of the present city. In 1848, in order to "give work to the populace and to embellish the city", the revolutionary government, presided over by Ruggero Settimo, decided to create a new main street by extending Via Maqueda from the plain di Sant'Oliva to the Colli plain; the new road was called Strada della Libertà. With the fall of the Bourbon monarchy and the proclamation of the unification of Italy, a city responsive to the needs and functional criteria of the rising entrepreneurial middle classes began to take shape. A new stratum of society was being formed from the beginning of the century and was given momentum by the presence of a colony of English families who had come to Sicily to establish an extremely prestigious wine business in the times of the alliance of the Bourbon court with England.

In 1840 the Florio family, entrepreneurs from Calabria who had moved to Sicily and

Left
The new building of the Villa Bordonaro, designed by Ernesto Basile at the end of the nineteenth century. Drawing by the architect.

Opposite
The façade of the nineteenth-century building of the villa.

were the owners of an economic empire with contacts in the world of finance and with the international intelligentsia, affiliated themselves with the Woodhouses and the Ingham-Whitakers. The Florios represented a new and sophisticated middle class which, connected by ties of kinship to the old aristocracy, took over the organization of the urban development of the city and brought it to the point where it could compete with the great centers of Europe. The announcement of an international competition for the design of the Teatro Massimo, a "monument of excellence" compulsory in every large European city, was a symbolic moment in this endeavor. The victory of an architect from Palermo, Giovan Battista Basile, attested to the level of taste and discernment in Palermo at that time.

Between the end of the nineteenth century and the beginning of the twentieth, Palermo attained the pinnacle of its fortunes. The year 1892 marked a moment of fundamental importance for the economic, cultural, and social life of the city. In that year the Sicilian capital was the seat of the Fourth National Exposition. This rehabilitated the south, within the general Italian context, from the points of view of agriculture, industry, and the arts.

The group of Sicilian medieval and Renaissance Revival buildings intended to house the exposition was designed by Ernesto Basile,

the son of Giovan Battista, who had, at the time, just succeeded to his chair at the university. The area selected was that of the old "firriato di Villafranca" situated along the Strada della Libertà between two of the main sites of the eighteenth-century city: the Teatro Politeama

Garibaldi and the Piazza delle Croci opposite the public garden, which was established between 1850 and 1851 in the English style, according to plans drawn up by Giovan Battista Basile.

At about this time Giovan Battista Basile also designed the nearby façade of the Reclusorio delle Croci in the neo-Gothic style; this was the stylistic prototype for the houses of the middle classes

that sprang up in the same area as the buildings of the national exposition.

Ernesto Basile devoted the first years of his work as an architect to a rediscovery of Sicilian styles as a key to the stylistic and cultural autonomy of the island; this was an almost symbolic conclusion to an entire century of local revivals – their beginnings, paradoxically, were owed to a Frenchman, Léon Dufourny, who championed the revival of the Doric order in the pavilion of the Botanical Garden. To the stylistic historicism of Basile were added the new concepts of European modernism and the awareness of the value of the traditions of local craftsmanship, which was at the heart of the planning of many buildings of the Art Nouveau period, initiated by Ernesto at the turn of the century with the construction of the Villino Florio and the Villa Igiea.

New building criteria were, in any case, already present in earlier structures, in which – according to the precepts of modernism – art and craftsmanship were for a time in perfect symbiosis. In the year after the Exposition, and in the very Piazza delle Croci where the buildings that had housed it stood, Ernesto Basile was appointed to rebuild and enlarge a building that had been acquired by the Chiaramonte-Bordonaro family, Baroni di Gebbiarossa.

Basile built the new villa in Florentine Renaissance style, with two floors divided verti-

cally by rusticated *lesene* (pilaster strips), windows with one and two lights on the second floor, a rectangular tower with windows on all four sides, and a projecting portico. He connected it to the old building on the upper floor via a passage in a gallery supported on corbels. The

old building is a rustic house on two floors, rectangular in plan, with two projecting wings and a raised terrace. He rendered this elevation with fake stucco bricks and cornices to match the style of the new building, which was faced with fired bricks and stone. Within the new building, an elegant staircase with wooden banisters leads from the entrance to the upper storey, where probably the most interesting room in the house is situated: a very beautiful library with elaborate wooden paneling and carvings, and with a coffered ceiling.

The architect also modernized the interiors of the old building. The reception rooms on the ground floor lead into one another *en enfilade* (in a row with all their doors aligned) in the part of the house that faced the old façade. The ballroom is in the centre; the clients ordered it to be decorated in neo seventeenth-century style and furnished it with pieces from the Palazzo Bordonaro ai Quattro Canti, including large Baroque mirrors with small landscapes painted in the upper panels of the frames. On the left, a door leads into the small Pompeian drawing room. A door on the right of the ballroom opens into a room with a ceiling painted with false coffering and grotesque motifs. A valuable collection of Hispano-Moresque ceramics was arranged along the upper part of the walls, alternating with garlands rendered in relief.

At the ends of the wings of the old building, symmetrically arranged around each of the two doors to the outside, three openings were adorned with Moorish horseshoe arches filled in with colored glass. The Villa Chiaramonte Bordonaro proclaims the new attitude of the "modernist" architect, who did not restrict his planning to the architecture alone but also concerned himself with furnishing the interiors, as well as arranging the beautiful wrought-iron gate and the cantilever roofs in iron and glass. This new idea of the role of the architect – which was already widespread in Europe and in England in particular – was sealed a few years later when Basile collaborated with the Ducrot furniture factory in one of the masterpieces of Art Nouveau in Italy, the Villa Igiea.

Right
The neo seventeenth-century ballroom in the old building, rebuilt by Ernesto Basile.

Casa Cuseni in Taormina

The ancient town of *Tauromenion* was founded in AD 358 by a group of Greek refugees from nearby Naxos, the earliest of the Greek colonies in Sicily. Under Roman domination, and, after a period of decline, it became, under Byzantine rule, the capital of eastern Sicily in place of Syracuse. It was conquered next by the Normans; although a few eminent feudal families lived in Taormina in the Aragonese period – including the Rosso and Palizzi families, who were responsible for a notable amount of building – Taormina suffered a long period of decline under Spanish domination. It recovered its self-respect only in the eighteenth century, when it came to be among the most fascinating places in Sicily to foreign travellers, who then disseminated their beguiling descriptions of its historic and natural riches.

Guy de Maupassant wrote: "A man who has only one day to spend in Sicily might ask, 'What must one see?' and I would answer without hesitating 'Taormina.' It is only a landscape, but a landscape in which one finds everything that seems to have been created on earth to captivate

Above
View of the façade of the Casa Cuseni, with the terraced garden in front.

Opposite
The garden of the villa with Mt. Etna under snow in the background.

the eyes, the spirit, and the imagination". Goethe wrote that: "No audience has ever had a spectacle before its eyes to equal the view from the seats of the theatre of Taormina ... two peaks joined by a semicircle ... the *skene* (stage), built across the foot of the stepped semicircle, connected the two rocky peaks, thus completing the most stupendous of all unions of nature and art ... to the right, castles rise on the higher rocky peaks, below lies the town ... now one sees, to the left of the entire long profile of Etna, the shore – as far as ... Syracuse; then the monstrous, smoking volcano closes the broad picture."

Sicily has always fascinated the English. Nelson, on whom Ferdinand of Bourbon had bestowed the dukedom of Bronte in eastern Sicily, unfortunately died before seeing his domain, where, it is said, he wanted to live out his days in peace. From 1890, Taormina was the center of the English community, a community of garden lovers. Lady Hill's garden in the old convent of Santa Caterina, and the garden with terraces covered in roses, above the church of San Giuseppe, were justly renowned. Florence Trevelyan's garden and that of Robert Hawthorn Kitson were also very well known. Kitson was twenty-seven when he came from Leeds to Taormina in 1900 to convalesce after an attack of rheumatic fever. He was so taken by the beauty of the area that

three years later he established his permanent residence there. A collector of paintings and works of art of various kinds – from Venetian glass to Persian ceramics and Sicilian madonnas – a connoisseur of contemporary English art and an excellent watercolorist himself, he designed a villa with a garden, which he called Casa Cuseni. He selected a steep hill outside the walls of the old town, from where he could simultaneously enjoy looking at the sea and the volcano: almost as good as the site of the ancient theatre.

The house was built in three years. Kitson took inspiration for its plans from Italian Renaissance villas, and Palladian villas in particular; he copied their simple rectangular plan, with two symmetrical wings that protrude slightly forwards, joined by a colonnade that supports a terrace. A spacious *salone* gives on to the colonnade along its entire length. Two square rooms flank it, one on each side. One of these, the most interesting room in the villa, was designed to be the dining room; it is a small masterpiece of the Arts and Crafts movement, which had started a few decades earlier in England with the object of promoting the applied arts to counteract the aesthetic poverty of objects in everyday use. The furniture and the paneling in light golden walnut in the dining room were designed in 1908 by Frank Brangwyn, an artist of Belgian origin who grew

up in London and had worked with William Morris. His allegorical wall paintings, dispersed through the whole world, had enjoyed great success. A great friend of Kitson's, as well as his teacher, Brangwyn painted a frieze on the upper part of the walls, with figures, fruit, and flowers during a second sojourn in Taormina.

The garden is of great distinction: influenced by the work of Sir Edwin Landseer Lutyens, the architect from London, it was laid out on terraces on several levels mounting steeply towards the villa, linked by flights of stairs, steps, and paths, strewn with terracotta jars, basins, and fountains with Rococo decorations. The most interesting part of the garden is on a hillock behind the house. It is paved with a mosaic of cobbles, following the practice of the Arts and Crafts movement, which encouraged the use of local materials and techniques. Although the technique of cobbling had flourished in the Baroque Tuscan gardens of the seventeenth century, it was also widely used in the following century in eastern Sicily, from Catania to Syracuse. A narrow path leads to the designer's masterpiece: a pool surrounded by pergolas, placed so that it reflects the summit of Etna.

The villa was requisitioned by the German army during the Second World War. It has since been the home of Robert Kitson's grand-daughter, the present owner, who has made it into a meeting place for philosophers, artists, writers and intellectuals.

Below and opposite
Paintings by Frank Brangwyn (*c.* 1910) on the walls of the dining room. The furniture of the dining room, in pale golden walnut, was also designed by Brangwyn.

Villino Caruso in Palermo

Palermo has been called a living museum of Art Nouveau. The Palermo exhibition of 1973, and the exposition *Palermo 1900* eight years later, helped to testify to the artistic importance of this period and to deepen the study of all those phenomena which, under the influence of the genius of Ernesto Basile,

PROSPETTO LATERALE A SINISTRA

formed this Palermo 'style' that had international significance. One example is the villino of the commendatore Vincenzo Caruso, on which building started in 1906. It was the only signed work of Filippo La Porta, an architect from Caltanissetta.

The only known details of La Porta's life concern the plans for the Florio tunny fishery on the island of Favignana. Here he collaborated with the better-known Giuseppe Damiani Almejda; he also probably worked for the Palermo furniture manufacturers Mucoli, building their factory in Piazza Croci. In 1892 La Porta signed a plan for the tomb of Gaetano Caruso, perhaps the father of the patron who built the Villino Caruso. It has been suggested that he collaborated with the architect Francesco Fichera, a pupil of Basile's, on the Villino Caruso. The outside of this building, which according to the critics is vaguely similar to the Villino Florio – which Basile completed in 1902 – reveals a solid, compact structure with rectangular windows on the raised first floor that is surrounded by a terrace, and tall, narrow windows on the upper story. The mass of the main part of the building is relieved by several square and polygonal towers.

La Porta's work was not confined to the architecture of the villino; it extended to the detailed design of the finishes and the furnishings. The raised first floor was reserved for reception rooms

Opposite
The spiral staircase in the turret.

Below
The spectacular turret that contains the stairwell.

arranged, with scrupulous attention to their function, around the great hall, with its coffered ceiling. Every coffer was filled with a circular brass ceiling lamp. The hall leads into the dining room – with wooden ceiling, paneling and fireplace — to the study, with walls covered in leather, and lastly, to a small drawing-room, also with wooden paneling. Several unpublished documents, included with the accounts for the building of the house, list the names of the suppliers of various materials used for the outside and the inside of the villa, the craftsmen who worked there and also provide information about later rebuilding.

During November 1908, the stonecutter Gioacchino Sammarco was paid for several jobs, including the carving of various pilasters in stone from the Isola delle Femmine and for a balcony around two façades of the house, made of the same stone, carved with balusters, plinth and cornice. In the same month the carpenter Gaetano Traviglia received payment for small finishing jobs "edge guards of Venetian wood, grooved, with rosettes and knots and finished by turning" while the *pittore adornista* (painter of embellishments) Domenico Denaro was paid for painting the decorative cornices in the minor rooms.

The finishing of the outside of the house, and more particularly the inside, was mostly done in 1909. In January,

Salvatore Martorella was paid for a certain amount of ironwork, including the banister for the spiral staircase, eight windows, and also certain railings and banisters "of complicated design" for which the firm of V. Hammeran supplied decorative roses and leaves. A "very large iron window" had

at that time already been supplied by the Oreta foundry.

In April, the firm of Giuseppe Carraffa supplied work in iron, copper and brass, faucets and various decorative objects, ceiling lamps and the hanging lamp in the *salone*. In May, the work

Opposite
The dining room with wainscotting and a coffered wooden ceiling.

Below
The great hall with a small veranda at the end.

of the cabinetmaker Giuseppe Zimmatore began: he made *boiserie* and the wooden paneling of the reception rooms, mostly in solid fir, with veneering and inlays of oak and maple. The ceiling of the study, on the other hand, was veneered in walnut with "moldings of beech from Trieste, polished and patinated with wax", while the painted leather work was done by Giuseppe La Manna.

Several documents attest to the work of Paolo Bevilacqua, which started in 1910, for the "painting, varnishing and artistic decoration" of various windows in the turret, the loggia, the belvedere, and above all, the main staircase. The lower part of this staircase is decorated with an interesting motif probably inspired by Tuscan and Roman examples of the late Renaissance, which, together with the decoration of the rooms, constitutes a distinctive interpretation of the tradition so dear to the poetic ideas of the early twentieth century.

Opposite
The walls of the study, covered in leather embossed with medieval motifs.

Below
The wooden corner fireplace in the dining room.

Below and opposite
The wooden staircase leading to
the private apartments: the lower
steps with a scroll motif probably
of Tuscan–Roman Mannerist
inspiration.

Following pages
The windows in the end wall of
the stairwell designed by Paolo
Bevilacqua in 1910.

Bibliography

ACCASCINA M., *Ottocento siciliano. Pittura*, Rome 1939.

ALBERTI L., *Descrittione di tutta Italia e Isole pertinenti ad essa di f. Leandro Alberti bolognese...*, Venice 1581.

ALESSI B., "Storia e architettura del Castello di Mussomeli", *Sicilia*, 73, 1973.

AMARI M., *Biblioteca Arabo-Sicula: raccolta di testi arabici che toccano la geografia*, Turin 1881.

AMARI M., *Storia dei Musulmani di Sicilia scritta da Michele Amari*, Palermo 1854–68.

AMICO V., *Dizionario topografico della Sicilia*, Palermo 1855.

BASILE N., *Palermo Felicissima. Divagazioni d'arte e di storia*, Palermo 1938.

BELLAFIORE G., *Architettura in Sicilia (1415–1535)*, Palermo 1984.

– *Architettura in Sicilia nell'età islamica e normanna (827–1194)*, Palermo 1990.

– *La Zisa di Palermo*, Palermo 1994.

BLUNT A., *Sicilian Baroque*, London 1968.

BOLOGNA F., *Il soffitto della Sala Magna allo Steri di Palermo e la cultura feudale siciliana nell'autunno del Medioevo*, Palermo 1975.

BORCH M. J., *Lettres sur la Sicile et sur l'Ile de Malthe de Monsieur de Borch...*, Turin 1782.

BOSCARINO S., *Sicilia barocca*, Rome 1986.

BOTTARI S., *Le arti figurative in Sicilia*, Messina 1954.

BRANCIFORTI O., *De Animorum Perturbationibus*, Catanae 1642.

BRYDONE P., *A Tour Through Sicily and Malta*, London 1773.

BURZOTTA P., "Dall'Orto Botanico al giardino del mondo: le opere di Léon Dufourny in Sicilia", *Lotus International*, 52, 1986.

CALANDRA R., LA MANNA A., SCUDERI V. e MALIGNAGGI D., *Palazzo dei Normanni*, Palermo 1991.

CANALE C. G., *Noto. La struttura continua della città tardo-barocca. Il potere di una società urbana nel Settecento*, Palermo 1976.

DAL CO F. and MAZZARIOL G., *Carlo Scarpa. Opera completa*, Milan 1984.

D'ALESSANDRO V. and GIARRIZZO G., *La Sicilia dal Vespro all'Unità d'Italia*, in *Storia d'Italia*, vol. XVI, Turin 1989.

DE BONIS A., *Ernesto Basile architetto*, Venice 1980.

DESCRIZIONE della Villa Valguarnera, Palermo 1785.

DE SETA C. and DI MAURO L., *Le città nella storia d'Italia. Palermo*, Bari, 1995.

DE SIMONE M., *Ville palermitane del XVII e XVIII secolo*. Genoa 1968.

– *VILLE palermitane dal XVI al XVIII secolo*, vol. II, Palermo 1974.

DI GIOVANNI V., *Palermo restaurato*, in *Biblioteca Storica e Letteraria di Sicilia* ed. by G. Di Marzo, Palermo 1872.

DI MARZO G., *Delle Belle Arti in Sicilia dai normanni sino alla fine del sec. XIV*, Palermo, 1858.

DI NATALE M. C., *Conoscere Palermo*, Palermo 1986.

DUFOURNY L., *Diario di un giacobino a Palermo 1789–93*, Palermo 1991.

EMMANUELE and GAETANI F. M. MARCHESE DI VILLABIANCA, *Della Sicilia Nobile*, Palermo 1754–1759.

– *PALERMO d'Oggigiorno*, ms. Qq D 162 in the Biblioteca Comunale di Palermo, sec. XVIII; pub. and ed. by G. Di Marzo in *Biblioteca Storica e Letteraria di Sicilia*, 1873–74.

FALCANDO U., "La historia o liber de regno Sicilie e l'epistola ad Petrus panormitane ecclesie thesaurarium", *Fonti per la storia d'Italia dell'Istituto storico italiano*, Rome 1897.

FAZELLO T., *De rebus siculis decades duae*, Panormi 1558; It. trans. by Remigio Fiorentino, Venice 1574.

FIDONE E. and SUSAN G., "Nuove acquisizioni filologiche su Luciano Alì (1736–1820)", in *Il Barocco in Sicilia tra conoscenza e conservazione*, ed. by di M. Fagiolo and L. Trigilia, Syracuse 1987.

GABRICI E. and LEVI E., *Lo Steri di Palermo e le sue pitture*, Milan 1932.

GANGI BATTAGLIA G. and VACCARO G., *Aquile sulle rocce*, Palermo 1968.

GARSTANG D., *Giacomo Serpotta and the stuccatori of Palermo*, London 1984.

GIARRIZZO G., "Il giardino itinerante delle passioni: le ville Branciforte (secolo XVII)", *Il giardino come labirinto della storia*, conference proceedings, Palermo 14–17 April 1984, Palermo 1987.

GIARRIZZO M. and ROTOLO A., *Mobili e mobilieri nella Sicilia del Settecento*, 1992

GIUFFRÈ M., *Castelli e luoghi forti di Sicilia XII–XVII secolo*, Palermo 1980.

– "La Casina Cinese di Palermo da Benedetto Lombardi a Ferdinando di Borbone", *Nel Regno delle Due Sicilie. Le cineserie*, Palermo 1994.

– "Dal Barocco al Neoclassicismo: Andrea Gigante architetto di frontiera", *Le arti in Sicilia nel Settecento. Studi in memoria di Maria Accascina*, Palermo 1985.

– "L'eredità di Giovanni Biagio Amico: note su Andrea Gigante e sullo scalone di Palazzo Bonagia in Palermo", *Giovanni Biagio Amico (1684–1754). Teologo, Architetto, Trattatista...*, Rome 1985.

GIUFFRIDA R. and CHIOVARO R., *La villa Whitaker a Malfitano*, Palermo 1986.

GIUFFRIDA R. and GIUFFRÈ M., *La Palazzina Cinese e il Museo Pitré nel Parco della Favorita a Palermo*, Palermo 1987.

GIUFFRIDA R., MALIGNAGGI D. e GRADITI S., *Nel palazzo dei Normanni di Palermo. La Sala d'Ercole*, Palermo 1987.

GOETHE J. W., *Italienische Reise*, Stuttgart and Tübingen, 1816–17.

GOLDSCHMIDT A., "Die normannischen Königspaläste in Palermo", *Zeitschrift für Bauwesen*, XLVIII, 1898.

GRASSO S., "Il palazzo Butera a Palermo: acquisizioni documentarie", *Antichità Viva*, 5, 1980.

GUTTILA M., *Monumenti e mito*, Palermo 1982.

HITTORFF J. J. and ZANTH L., *Architecture moderne de la Sicile*, Paris 1835.

HONOUR H., *L'arte della della cineseria*, Florence, 1963.

HOUEL J. P. L. L., *Voyage pittoresque des îles de Sicile, de Malte et de Lipari*, Paris 1782–87.

HOWELL S., "The view from Miss Phelps' bed", *The world of interiors*, 11, 1990.

IBN GUBAYR, *Viaggio in Ispagna, Sicilia, Siria e Palestina, Mesopotamia, Arabia, Egitto*, C. Schiaparelli, ed., Palermo 1979.

IDRISI, *Il libro di Ruggero. Il diletto di chi è appassionato per le peregrinazioni attraverso il mondo*, Palermo 1994.

KRONIG W., "Il Palazzo reale normanno della Zisa a Palermo. Nuove osservazioni", *Commentarii*, 3–4, 1977.

LA DUCA R., *Bagli, casene e ville della piana dei Colli*, Palermo 1965.

– *Repertorio bibliografico degli edifici pubblici e privati di Palermo*, Palermo 1994.

LANZA DI TRABIA S., *Gnovissima guida pel viaggiatore in Sicilia*, Palermo 1884.

LANZA TOMASI G., *Castelli e Monasteri di Sicilia*, Palermo 1968.

– *Le ville di Palermo*, Palermo 1965.

LEANTI A., *Lo stato presente della Sicilia*, Palermo 1761.

LOMBARDO A., "I Whitaker e villa Malfitano", in '*Nuovi quaderni del Meridione*', 97–98, 1987.

LO JACONO G., *Studi e rilievi di palazzi palermitani dell'età barocca*, Palermo 1962.

LIBRANDO V., *Palazzo Biscari in Catania*, Catania 1965.

MANIACI A., "La Domus Magna di Guglielmo Ajutamicristo: vicende costruttive e sua paternità", *Storia Architettura*, 1–2, 1986.

MAUPASSANT G. DE, *La vie errante*, Palermo 1977.

MAURO E., *Le ville a Palermo*, Palermo 1992.

MELI F., "Degli architetti del Senato di Palermo nei secoli XVII–XVIII", *Archivio Storico Siciliano*, 4, 1938–39.

MORSO S., *Descrizione di Palermo Antico ricavata sugli autori sincroni e i monumenti de' tempi da Salvadore Morso*, Palermo 1827.

Il Palazzo del Governo di Palermo. Ampliamento e restauro del palazzo Comitini, Palermo 1931.

NEIL E. H., *Architecture in Context: The Villas of Bagheria, Sicily*, PhD Dissertation Harvard University, 1995

PALAZZOLO GRAVINA V., *Genealogia della famiglia Termine e sue relazioni*, Palermo 1875.

PALERMO G., *Guida istruttiva per potersi conoscere con facilità tanto dal Siciliano che dal Forestiero tutte le magnificienze e gli oggetti degni di nota della città di Palermo*, Palermo 1816.

PERI I., *La Sicilia dopo il Vespro. Uomini, città e campagne 1282–1376*, Bari 1982.

– *UOMINI, città e campagne in Sicilia dall'XI al XIII secolo*, Bari 1978.

PIAZZA S. and SCADUTO F., "Dal cortile allo scalone. Gli spazi della celebrazione nei palazzi nobiliari di Palermo", *L'uso dello spazio privato nell'età dell'Illuminismo* a cura di G. Simoncini, Florence 1995.

PIOLA C., *Dizionario delle strade di Palermo preceduto da una corsa per Palermo e i suoi dintorni*, Palermo 1994.

PIRRONE G., *Palermo, una capitale. Dal Settecento al Liberty*, Milan 1989.

PIRRONE G., BUFFA M., MAURO E. and SESSA E., "*Palermo, detto Paradiso di Sicilia*" (Ville e Giardini, XII–XX secolo), Palermo, 1989.

PIRRONE G. and COSENTINI G. G., *Donnafugata. Un castello un giardino*.

PITINI V., "Palazzi e ville di Palermo nel periodo della decadenza", *Nuova Antologia di Scienze, Lettere ed Arti*, 163, 1913.

PRESCIA R., "L'attuale palazzo Ajutamicristo a Palermo: l'organismo architettonico", in *Storia Architettura*, 1–2, 1986.

QUEST-RITSON C., *The English Garden Abroad*, London 1996.

RANZANO P., *Delle origini e vicende di Palermo*, Palermo, 1864 [*Opusculum de auctore primordiis et progressu felicis urbis Panormi, nunc primum in lucem prodiit*, Panormi 1753].

REQUIREZ S. *Le ville di Palermo*, Palermo 1996.

ROMUALDO SALERNITANO, "Chronicon", C. A. Garufi ed. in *Rerum Italicarum Scriptores*, Bologna 1928.

ROTOLO F., *Matteo Carnilivari. Revisione e Documenti*, Palermo, 1985.

SAINT NON J. C. R. DE, *Voyage pittoresque, ou Description des Royames de Naples et de Sicile*, Paris 1781–1786.

SALVO BARCELLONA G., "Il lavoro degli artigiani del Settecento nel palazzo Comitini", in *Le arti in Sicilia nel Settecento. Studi in memoria di Maria Accascina*, Palermo 1985.

– *Il palazzo Comitini*, Palermo 1981.

SAN MARTINO DE SPUCCHES F., *Storia dei feudi e dei titoli nobiliari di Sicilia dalla loro origine ai nostri giorni*, Palermo 1927.

SANTORO R., "Considerazioni generali sull'evoluzione delle fortificazioni siciliane dall'ultima amministrazione imperiale bizantina al consolidamento del regno di Sicilia", *Archivio Storico Siciliano*, 1976.

– *La Sicilia dei castelli. La difesa dell'isola dal VI al XVIII secolo. Storia e architettura*, Palermo 1986.

SARULLO L., *Dizionario degli artisti siciliani*, Palermo 1993–1994.

SCIASCIA L. and LA DUCA R., *Palermo Felicissima*, Palermo 1973.

SIRACUSA urbs magnificentissima. La collezione Beneventano di Monteclimiti, catalogo della mostra, Milan 1994.

SIRACUSANO C., *La Pittura del Settecento in Sicilia*, Rome, 1986.

SORGE G., *Mussomeli. Dall'origine all'abolizione della feudalità*, Catania 1910.

SPATRISANO G., *Lo Steri di Palermo e l'architettura siciliana del Trecento*, Palermo 1972.

STELLA E., *La lunga vita di palazzo Ajutamicristo*, in ALFANO N., *Breve storia della casa. Osservazioni sui tipi abitativi e la città*, Rome.

TEDESCO N., *Villa Palagonia*, Palermo 1988.

TOBRINER S., *The Genesis of Noto*, Berkeley 1982.

TREVELYAN R., *Principi sotto il vulcano*, Milan 1977.

VENTURI A., *Storia dell'arte italiana. Dai primordi dell'arte cristiana all'architettura del Cinquecento*, Milan, 1901–1940.

ZIINO V., *Contributi allo studio dell'Architettura del '700 in Sicilia*, Palermo 1950.

Addresses
of the palazzi

Palazzo Reale
Piazza Parlamento 1,
Palermo
can be visited by appointment

Castello della Zisa
Piazza Zisa 1, Palermo
open to the public

**Palazzo Chiaramonte
detto lo Steri**
Piazza Marina 61, Palermo
can be visited by appointment

Castello Chiaramonte
Contrada Castello,
Mussomeli (Caltanissetta)
open to the public

Palazzo Termine-Pietratagliata
Via Bandiera 14, Palermo
closed to the public

Palazzo Aiutamicristo
Via Garibaldi 23, Palermo
closed to the public

Villa San Marco
Via San Marco 90,
Santa Flavia (Palermo)
closed to the public

Villa De Simone-Wirz
Via Apollo 44, Palermo
closed to the public

Palazzo Butera
Via Butera, Palermo
closed to the public

Villa Valguarnera
Via Gramsci, Bagheria
(Palermo)
closed to the public

Villa Palagonia
Piazza Garibaldi, Bagheria
(Palermo)
open to the public

Palazzo Valguarnera-Gangi
Piazza Croce dei Vespri 6,
Palermo
closed to the public

Palazzo Biscari
Via Museo Biscari 10,
Catania
closed to the public

Palazzo Comitini
Via Maqueda 100, Palermo
closed to the public

Villa Camastra-Tasca
Corso Calatafimi 446,
Palermo
closed to the public

Palazzo Trigona di Canicarao
Via Cavour 93, Noto
(Syracuse)
closed to the public

Palazzo Beneventano del Bosco
Piazza Duomo, Siracusa
closed to the public

Villa Ajroldi
Piazza Leoni 9, Palermo
closed to the public

Villa Spedalotto
Via De Spuches, Bagheria
(Palermo)
closed to the public

Palazzina Cinese
Via Duca degli Abruzzi,
Palermo
open to the public

Castello di Donnafugata
Contrada Donnafugata,
Ragusa
open to the public

Villa Whitaker
Via Dante 167, Palermo
open to the public

Villa Bordonaro alle Croci
Via delle Croci 7, Palermo
closed to the public

Casa Cuseni
Via Leonardo da Vinci 7,
Taormina (Messina)
closed to the public

Villino Caruso
Via Dante 159, Palermo
closed to the public

Index of names and places

The names of villas, palazzi and castles dealt with in detail are in capitals.